The Brontës

Pocket BIOGRAPHIES

Series Editor C.S. Nicholls

Highly readable brief lives of those who have played a significant part in history, and whose contributions still influence contemporary culture.

Pocket BIOGRAPHIES

The Brontës

KATHRYN WHITE

SUTTON PUBLISHING

First published in 1998 by
Sutton Publishing Limited · Phoenix Mill
Thrupp · Stroud · Gloucestershire · GL5 2BU

British Library Cataloguing in Publication Data

A catalogue record for this book is available from the British Library

ISBN 0-7509-1931-0

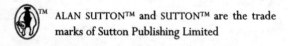

ALAN SUTTON™ and SUTTON™ are the trade
marks of Sutton Publishing Limited

Typeset in 13/18pt Perpetua.
Typesetting and origination by
Sutton Publishing Limited.
Printed in Great Britain by
The Guernsey Press Company Limited,
Guernsey, Channel Islands.

For Mum, Dad and David

C O N T E N T S

ACKNOWLEDGEMENTS

I am grateful to the British Library, the National Portrait Gallery and the Brontë Society for permission to use photographs from their collections, and to the staff of the Brontë Parsonage Museum past and present, particularly to Ann Dinsdale for all her help in recent years.

No work on the Brontës could be written today without acknowledging an enormous debt to the monumental scholarly work of Margaret Smith and Juliet Barker, whose books must be the benchmark for any serious study of the Brontës.

Finally thanks to my editor, Christine Nicholls, for her tolerance and advice, and to my unofficial editor, whose tolerant support constantly amazes me, my husband David Stuart Davies.

CHRONOLOGY

1777	**17 March**. The Brontës' father, Patrick Brontë, born at Emdale, County Down, Ireland.
1783	**15 April**. The Brontës' mother, Maria Branwell, born at Penzance, Cornwall.
1812	**29 December**. Patrick Brontë marries Maria Branwell, Guiseley Church, near Leeds.
1814	Their first child, Maria Brontë, born at Hartshead, Yorkshire. Baptized at Hartshead, 23 April.
1815	**8 February**. Elizabeth Brontë born at Hartshead.
1816	**21 April**. Charlotte Brontë born at Thornton, near Bradford, Yorkshire.
1817	**26 June**. Patrick Branwell Brontë born at Thornton.
1818	**30 July**. Emily Jane Brontë born at Thornton.
1820	**17 January**. Their sixth and last child, Anne Brontë, born at Thornton.
	February. Patrick appointed perpetual curate of St Michael and All Angels Church, Haworth, near Keighley, Yorkshire. The family move to Haworth in April.
1821	**15 September**. Mrs Maria Brontë dies, aged thirty-eight.

1824   **July**. Maria and Elizabeth sent to the Clergy Daughters' School at Cowan Bridge, near Kirby Lonsdale, followed by Charlotte in August and Emily in November.

1825   **February**. Maria falls ill at Cowan Bridge and dies at home on 6 May. Elizabeth falls ill and is withdrawn from the school, as are Charlotte and Emily. Elizabeth dies at home on 15 June.

1825–31   The remaining four children educated at home by their father and aunt.

1831   **January**. Charlotte attends Roe Head School, Mirfield, run by the Misses Wooler. Meets her lifelong friends Ellen Nussey and Mary Taylor.

1832   **June**. Charlotte teaches her sisters at home before returning to Roe Head from July 1835 to December 1838 as a teacher. Emily accompanies her as a free pupil but leaves after a few months, suffering from severe homesickness, and is replaced by Anne, who remains until December 1838.

1838   **June**. Branwell sets up as a portrait painter in Bradford but returns home in debt, May 1839.

    September. Emily is a teacher at Law Hill school, Halifax, for six months.

1839   **April**. Anne is governess to the Inghams of Blake Hall, Mirfield, Yorkshire; leaves December 1839.

    May. Charlotte is governess to the Sidgwicks of Stonegappe, Lothersdale; leaves July 1839.

1840   **January**. Branwell is tutor to the Postlethwaites, Broughton-in-Furness; leaves June 1840.

1840   **May**. Anne is governess to the Robinsons of Thorp Green, Little Ouseburn, near York; leaves June 1845.

September. Branwell is clerk on the new railway at Sowerby Bridge, near Halifax.

1841   **March**. Charlotte is governess to the Whites of Upperwood House, Rawdon, near Leeds; leaves December 1841.

April. Branwell promoted to clerk-in-charge at Luddenden Foot station, near Halifax, but is dismissed in April 1842 for negligence in keeping the accounts.

1842   **February**. Charlotte and Emily study in Brussels at the Pensionnat Heger but are called back when Aunt Branwell dies on 29 October 1842.

1843   **January**. Branwell joins Anne at Thorp Green as tutor. Charlotte returns to Brussels alone and develops a deep admiration for her married professor, Constantin Heger.

1844   **January**. Charlotte returns to Haworth from Brussels.

1845   **June**. Anne leaves Thorp Green. Branwell dismissed from Thorp Green in July after the discovery of a relationship between him and his employer's wife, Lydia Robinson.

Autumn. Charlotte discovers Emily's poems and the three sisters prepare to publish a selection of their poems, to appear under pseudonyms.

1846   **May**. *Poems* by Currer, Ellis and Acton Bell published by Aylott & Jones.

1847   **16 October**. *Jane Eyre* published by Smith Elder & Co.

        December. *Wuthering Heights* and *Agnes Grey* published by T.C. Newby.

1848   **May**. Anne's second novel, *The Tenant of Wildfell Hall*, published.

        July. Anne and Charlotte travel to London to meet their publishers and dispel the rumours surrounding their authorship.

        24 September. Death of Branwell at Haworth, aged thirty-one.

        19 December. Death of Emily at Haworth, aged thirty.

1849   **28 May**. Death of Anne at Scarborough, aged twenty-nine.

        October. Publication of Charlotte's second novel, *Shirley*.

1850–1   On visits to London Charlotte meets authors William Makepeace Thackeray and Harriet Martineau, and sits for portrait by George Richmond. Meets Elizabeth Gaskell in the Lake District. Edits new edition of *Wuthering Heights* and *Agnes Grey*. Visits Great Exhibition of 1851.

1853   **January**. Publication of Charlotte's third novel, *Villette*.

1854   **29 June**. Charlotte marries Arthur Bell Nicholls, her father's curate, at Haworth.

1855   **31 March**. Charlotte dies, aged thirty-eight, in the early stages of pregnancy. Mr Nicholls remains at Haworth to look after Mr Brontë.

1857   **March**. Publication of *The Life of Charlotte Brontë* by Elizabeth Gaskell and posthumous publication of Charlotte's first novel, *The Professor*.

1861   **7 June**. Patrick Brontë, the last survivor of his family, dies aged eighty-four. Mr Nicholls goes home to Ireland.

1893   **16 December**. Foundation of the Brontë Society.

1897   **26 November**. Death of Ellen Nussey, aged eighty.

1901   Death of George Smith, Charlotte's publisher.

1906   **2 December**. Death of Arthur Bell Nicholls, aged eighty-eight.

INTRODUCTION

The Brontës are the world's most remarkable literary family, their parsonage home in Haworth, on the edge of the Yorkshire moors, nurturing not just one but three writers of genius. Charlotte, Emily and Anne Brontë wrote some of the greatest novels in the English language. Charlotte's passionate *Jane Eyre* and Emily's powerful *Wuthering Heights* have never been out of print since their first publication over a hundred and fifty years ago in 1847. Anne's *The Tenant of Wildfell Hall* is a direct analysis of alcoholism and domestic cruelty, and the sisters' novels are among the top-selling classics of all time.

The Brontës' solitary lives and tragically early deaths have become a part of the legends of English literature. Published under the pseudonyms of Currer, Ellis and Acton Bell, their books invited intense scrutiny. Were they one author or several? Men or women? An American reviewer, believing the Bells to be just one person, commented, 'there is nothing kindly or genial in the author's powerful mind . . . if he continues to write novels, he will introduce into the land of romance a larger number of hateful men and women than any other writer of the day'.[1] Were the Bells men or women?

Whatever reservations the critics may have had, when *Jane Eyre* was first published it was an immediate and enormous popular success. One of the first reviews stated, 'It is a book to make the pulses gallop and the heart beat, and to fill the eyes with tears'.[2] All of literary London speculated as to the identity of the mysterious Currer Bell and while most critics acknowledged the novel's power and originality, some attacked its perceived coarseness and brutality. Meanwhile the author, a 31-year-old clergyman's daughter, sat in her quiet home at Haworth, reading the reviews with her two younger sisters, Emily and Anne, whose novels *Wuthering Heights* and *Agnes Grey* were to reach the bookshelves two months later and be subjected to similar praise of their uncompromising strength and criticism of their vulgarity.

The Brontës' identities emerged gradually but it was not until 1850, after the deaths of Emily, who guarded her privacy jealously, and Anne that it became common knowledge in Haworth that the parson's daughters were famous authors. Charlotte described the reaction of the parsonage's young servant, Martha Brown:

> Martha came in yesterday – puffing and blowing and much excited – 'I've heard sich news,' she began – 'What about?' 'Please ma'am, you've been and written two books, the grandest books that ever was seen. My Father has heard it at Halifax, and Mr George Taylor and Mr Greenwood, and Mr Merrall at Bradford; and they are going to have a meeting at the Mechanics' Institute, and to settle about ordering them.' 'Hold your tongue, Martha, and be off.' I fell into a cold sweat. 'Jane Eyre' will be read by John Brown, by Mrs Taylor, and Betty. God help, keep, and deliver me!'[3]

A few days later the first of the many millions of tourists to visit Haworth arrived in the village but Charlotte reassured her publishers that 'our rude hills and rugged neighbourhood will I doubt not form a sufficient barrier to the frequent repetition of such visits'.[4] The excitement and fascination engendered by the Brontës' novels has not diminished in the intervening years. Their novels have been translated into dozens of different languages and have been dramatized hundreds of times across the world.

A 'pocket biography' can only touch upon the highlights of the Brontës' lives, for we are dealing with three members of a close-knit family of writers in a limited number of words. There are many biographies and studies devoted to the Brontës and I have listed some of the most significant in the bibliography. This book is intended to distill the essence of the Brontës and provide the key to a deeper interest and an enthusiasm for the lives and works of the world's most remarkable literary family.

As an early review of *Jane Eyre* commented, 'the book is closed, the enchantment continues . . .'.[5] The characters that sprang from Haworth have a life beyond the printed page. When we read or re-read the Brontës' novels, study their lives, or visit their former home, now the Brontë Parsonage Museum, and breathe in the sharp air of the bleak surrounding moorlands, we are drawn in by that enchantment. Let the Brontës cast their spell.

ONE

FORMATIVE INFLUENCES, 1777–1820

The Brontës are perceived as being inseparable from the Yorkshire moors where they lived but although they spent all their lives in the county, it is often forgotten that their genetic inheritance was Celtic; their father was Irish and their mother Cornish. However, since Mrs Brontë died before Charlotte, the eldest surviving child, was six years old, the major influence on their lives and creativity was their father, the Revd Patrick Brontë. He has often been portrayed as a stern, authoritarian figure, a picture coloured by how the first Brontë biographer, the novelist Elizabeth Gaskell, whose *The Life of Charlotte Brontë* was published in 1857, viewed his character. The truth, as has been shown many times since, is very different – yet the myth persists.

Patrick Brontë was a supportive and liberal father, a man of remarkable determination and ambition who, through his own exertions, rose from his beginnings in rural Ireland to become a respected clergyman and the father of genius. Born on St Patrick's Day in 1777 into a poor family, he was the eldest of the ten children of Hugh Brontë and his wife Eleanor (sometimes known as Alice) McClory. The family's original name is uncertain and is listed in Irish records variously as 'Brunty' and 'Bruntee'.[1] Patrick spent his early years in Emdale, County Down, Ireland, and at the age of sixteen he became a teacher in the local school. His ability attracted the attention of an influential local clergyman, the Revd Thomas Tighe, an Evangelical and a graduate of St John's College, Cambridge, and Patrick became tutor to his children. In 1802, in his mid-twenties, he became a sizar at St John's College, Cambridge, where he studied Classics. It was probably while he was at Cambridge that Patrick changed his name from 'Brunty' to 'Brontë'. The reasons are unclear but may be connected with some confusion over Patrick's Irish accent. The entry registers at St John's College record his name as 'Pranty' and not long afterwards Patrick's signature is listed as 'Brontë',[2] possibly emulating his hero, the naval legend Horatio Nelson, who had become Duke of Bronte, in Sicily, in 1799.

Today, it is difficult for us to appreciate the vast social leap that Patrick had made in entering Cambridge University, one of the cornerstones of the English class system. As a sizar among the wealthy and the scions of aristocracy, Patrick paid reduced fees and was marked out by his Irish accent and humble background. He had achieved his position through hard work and intellectual ability. He recognized education as a means to advancement for the poor and he was to instil in his children the same values. Many years later, he and his family were noted for their kind treatment of their servants and his daughters' novels burn with a sense of the injustices of society.

Patrick's time at Cambridge was marked by diligence and academic success and he struggled to manage on his meagre funds, teaching pupils to earn extra money. His remarkable rise drew him to the attention of such well-known figures as William Wilberforce, who was one of several people to sponsor Patrick's progression through university. St John's was primarily a clerical college with

Evangelical leanings and Patrick was now encouraged to choose a career in the church. He had a missionary zeal and was an ardent and practical Christian rather than one who would seek a comfortable parish for its social cachet. There is often a misconception that his religion was harsh, even Calvinist, in outlook but it is clear from Patrick's surviving writings[3] that he preached a kindly doctrine in which sinners would be forgiven and go to Heaven, rather than the Doctrine of the Elect taught by the Calvinists. His daughter Anne also favoured the view of a benevolent God espoused by the Universal Salvationists in both her life and her fiction, particularly in *The Tenant of Wildfell Hall*,[4] in which Helen Huntingdon tries to reassure her dissolute and fatally ill husband that God will forgive him.

By 1806 Patrick was ordained in the Church of England and took up his first position at Wethersfield in Essex, before becoming a fully fledged clergyman in December 1807. He then progressed through a succession of curacies at Wellington in Shropshire and Dewsbury, Yorkshire, before finding himself at Hartshead-cum-Clifton, on the hillside between Halifax, Brighouse and

Bradford. While there, his Classical education provided him with the additional responsibility of being an examiner in Classics at Woodhouse Grove School, near Bradford. Here he met his future wife, Maria Branwell, the 29-year-old daughter of a Penzance merchant, Thomas Branwell, and his wife, Anne Carne. Maria was the niece by marriage of the headmaster of Woodhouse Grove, John Fennell, a friend of the Revd William Morgan, with whom Patrick had shared duties at Wellington. At this time, Patrick was in his mid-thirties, a tall, handsome man with auburn hair. He had no family income, just his slender salary as a curate, while Maria came from a comfortable middle-class background. It is clear that theirs was very much a love match. She wrote to Patrick during their courtship, 'the anticipation of sharing with you all the pleasures and pains, the cares and anxieties of life, of contributing to your comfort and becoming the companion of your pilgrimage, is more delightful to me than any other prospect which this world can possibly present'.[5]

Long after her mother's death, Patrick gave their daughter Charlotte some of Maria's letters to read, an experience which she found incredibly moving.

In one of these letters Maria addresses her fiancé as 'My dear Saucy Pat', and she reveals a playful and firm character with an excellent command of language.[6] Their marriage took place on 29 December 1812. It was a joint wedding, with William Morgan marrying Maria's cousin, Jane Branwell Fennell, on the same day and each groom performing the wedding ceremony for the other. Patrick and Maria Brontë set up home together at Lousy Thorn, Hartshead, and then at Clough House, Hightown. Their first child, Maria, was born at Clough House. The date of her birth is not known but she was baptized on 23 April 1814, and a second daughter, Elizabeth, followed on 8 February 1815.

Soon after Elizabeth's birth, the family moved to Thornton, near Bradford in Yorkshire, and occupied the parsonage at Market Street. It was here that Charlotte, Emily and Anne were born in 1816, 1818 and 1820 respectively. The only boy in the family, Patrick Branwell, was born in 1817. The Brontës made friends with the family of Elizabeth Firth, who kept a diary[7] in which she made notes of all the comings and goings of Thornton life. It reveals that this was a very happy time for the Brontës. Patrick and Maria were deeply in love, they had a growing young family, kind friends, and Patrick was already a published author.

Unfavourable comparisons have often been made between Patrick's writings and those of his children but it has to be remembered that he was writing for a completely different audience. Patrick's first collection of poetry, *Cottage Poems* (1811), reflected his own Evangelical zeal for learning and disseminating the message of Christ. He was passionate about seeing poor folk improving their lot and his poems were 'designed for the lower classes of society', aiming at 'simplicity, plainness, and perspicuity, both in manner and style';[8] he did not intend to create great literature. Patrick's poetry is sometimes clumsy and clichéd, but he had the enthusiasm and the ability to write. He produced several collections of poetry and tales between 1811 and 1818,[9] all with a similar readership in mind. His children were to grow up in a book-loving environment which valued education and debate. Maria Brontë also wrote. A manuscript religious tract of hers, fairly conventional and intended for publication, discusses 'The Advantages of Poverty in Religious Concerns',[10] and Patrick kept it as a memorial to his wife.

Patrick was keen to advance his career further and in 1819 the Bishop of Bradford offered him the perpetual curacy of St Michael and All Angels Church at Haworth, eight miles away, which was vacant after the death of the Revd James Charnock. However, the Church Trustees had an ancient right to elect their own minister and though they had no objection to Patrick personally, they claimed the right to choose. Patrick kept out of the ensuing negotiations as much as possible and he and other clergymen filled in the duties at Haworth until Patrick was finally accepted there in February 1820.

In April the Brontës left Thornton behind and headed for a new life with their young servants from Thornton, the sisters Nancy and Sarah Garrs. The children, Maria, Elizabeth, Charlotte, Branwell, Emily and Anne, were aged from seven to one year old, and the youngest four would retain few memories of Thornton. For them, Haworth was to be their home for the rest of their lives.

EARLY LIFE AT HAWORTH, 1820–31

In contrast to their home at Thornton, which was situated in the village centre, the parsonage at Haworth was a little larger, with a garden, and set on the edge of the township, backing on to open moorland. The front of the Georgian parsonage, built in 1779, faced the church and was surrounded on two sides by the graves in the overcrowded churchyard.

Despite the wave of industrialization and scientific thought that had begun to sweep the country, the sanitary conditions in Haworth and many other parts of Britain were still practically medieval in 1821. Haworth was an extremely unhealthy place to live, the average age of death being just twenty-five, and forty-one per cent of the population died before reaching the age of six. Conditions were as bad as those in the worst slums of London. It was not until 1850, after representations from Mr Brontë and a group of concerned local people, that an inspector from London examined health and sanitation in Haworth.[1] His report makes shocking reading. Although it was the norm for there to be no indoor plumbing, in Haworth there was an average of just one outside toilet, known as a privy or earth closet, to every 4.5 houses. In one instance twenty-four homes shared one privy. The soiled earth from the privies was carried away by the 'nightsoil man' but some of the effluent ran down the main street and midden heaps of refuse were stacked against kitchen windows, increasing the risk of cross-infection. The chapelry of Haworth had a population of 6,303 in 1850, with an average of 5.09 people living in each dwelling. The main water supply for Haworth ran underneath the churchyard and was polluted by the decomposing corpses. Fortunately the Parsonage water supply came from a well behind the house which was not affected. The graveyard itself had seen some 1,344 burials in the space of just ten years and many of the tombs were covered by a horizontal slab of stone that did not admit air and prevented the gases formed by decomposition from escaping properly, creating an unpleasant miasma around the churchyard. The 1850 report resulted in many recommendations, including the planting of trees to aid the decomposition process, but it was not until after the Brontë period that most of them were implemented. It is no wonder that Charlotte Brontë was so frequently plagued by headaches and nausea. Although the Brontës' early deaths were indeed tragic – none of the six Brontë children reached the age of forty – such losses were not uncommon in Haworth, and in nineteenth-century England. Indeed, the Brontës benefited from living in more spacious accommodation than the majority of the population, which probably helped to prolong their lives.

Haworth is eight hundred feet above sea level, with nothing behind it but the Pennine hills. In winter the Parsonage, unprotected by the trees that now surround it, was buffeted by the winds on every side. The children loved to walk regularly on the moors, which Emily described in the opening chapter of *Wuthering Heights*:

Pure, bracing ventilation they must have up there, at all times, indeed: one may guess the power of the north wind, blowing over the edge, by the excessive slant of a few, stunted firs at the end of the house; and by a range of gaunt thorns all stretching their limbs one way, as if craving alms of the sun.[2]

Cold and ill health punctuated their lives, yet the family all loved their home. Emily in particular suffered dreadful homesickness if she was away for any length of time. These stanzas are taken from a poem written when she was a teacher at Law Hill school:

> There is a spot 'mid barren hills
> Where winter howls and driving rain,
> But if the dreary tempest chills
> There is a light that warms again.
>
> The house is old, the trees are bare
> And moonless bends the misty dome
> But what on earth is half so dear,
> So longed for as the hearth of home?[3]

Nineteenth-century Haworth was a tough place but Elizabeth Gaskell portrayed its people as rude savages, basing much of her description on accounts dating back to the eighteenth century. Depicting the authors' surroundings as bleak and uncivilized added weight to her defence of the reputations of Charlotte and her sisters. Gaskell felt she had a mission to protect the Brontës' personal morality from the accusations of coarseness and brutality that had been directed at their novels. If she suggested that the Brontës merely wrote about the violence and amorality of those around them, their own reputations would remain intact. This perception of Charlotte, the dutiful heroine in adverse surroundings, also tainted Gaskell's view of Mr Brontë, whom she represented as distant from his children and wildly eccentric, when in reality he cared deeply about his family and was merely unconventional.

The majority of the people in Haworth were unlearned but the township was not the social backwater Gaskell would have had her readers believe. Situated close to the Lancashire border, Haworth saw a great deal of passing traffic and had several inns, a clutch of textile mills, and thriving local societies and musical events. Haworth is four miles from the nearest large town, Keighley, and over twice as far again from other centres of population such as Halifax, Bradford and Leeds. The

Brontës were not wealthy enough to own a carriage or a horse and there was only one small cart for hire in Haworth, which made any journey beyond walking distance both expensive and time-consuming. The railway came to Keighley in 1847 but did not reach Haworth until after the Brontës lived there.

Haworth was full of people and activity but remote from the kind of intellectual stimulation craved by the Brontë family. There were people in the village who were wealthier than the Brontës but few who had their thirst for knowledge. It was an intellectual isolation which Branwell and Charlotte especially found hard to cope with. Emily and Anne seem to have been more self-sufficient.

The Brontës' environment affected their work deeply and it is interesting to contrast the work and surroundings of Elizabeth Gaskell, whose life in rural Cheshire and in Manchester, a thriving industrial city, is reflected in a much more socially integrated approach to her novels. Similarly, a comparison of the Brontës' and Gaskell's handwriting shows the three Brontës expressing a neat, angular, precisely controlled passion, whereas Gaskell's hand is cursive, free-flowing and open.

The Brontës had little opportunity to settle into their new home, for not long after their arrival, Mrs Brontë became ill with suspected internal cancer in January 1821. While still coming to terms with his new position and the duties of a large parish, Mr Brontë had to cope with not only his dear wife's confinement to bed but also being a stranger to Haworth and having financial worries. He spared no expense in seeking treatment for Maria and fell into debt. Fortunately friends and colleagues anticipated his problems and he received sums of money to help, all of which he paid back in better times.

Mrs Brontë's death was lingering and painful, her illness lasting over seven months. She had told Patrick during their courtship that she sometimes felt that she was more attached to earth than to heaven, a sentiment echoed by Catherine Earnshaw in *Wuthering Heights*. As she lay dying, the dilemma manifested itself in a temporary lack of faith and an acute concern as to what would become of her children after her death. The servants remembered hearing their mistress crying out continually, 'Oh God my poor children – oh God my poor children!'[4] Nancy and Sarah, though caring and good workers, were only young girls and for a time Mrs Brontë had a nurse, who was later sent away for reasons that are unclear. Interviewed by Elizabeth Gaskell in the 1850s, this 'good old woman' may have borne a grudge and was the source of the tales of Mr Brontë's eccentric behaviour which appeared in the *Life*. It was a huge comfort to Mr Brontë when Maria's older unmarried sister, Elizabeth Branwell, travelled from Cornwall to look after the invalid.

Mrs Brontë died at the age of thirty-eight on 15 September 1821. Patrick was heartbroken and did not resume his duties for a week after her death. He now had to cope with a demanding job, low income and the needs of six small children. Aunt Branwell, as she became known, remained to care for the children, but naturally she could not fill the space left by her sister. Charlotte's only memory of her mother was a dim recollection of her nursing Branwell in the dining room. Aunt Branwell, and later their older servant, Tabitha Aykroyd, who joined the family in 1825, between them fulfilled different elements of a mother's role. The fastidious Aunt Branwell, who wore wooden overshoes known as pattens indoors to protect her feet from the cold stone floors of the Parsonage, provided instruction in needlework and the elementary aspects of the female 'accomplishments', while Tabby's cosy kitchen and broad Yorkshire accent offered an alternately warm, scolding and practical motherliness as well as a fund of local stories and gossip for the ears of the eager children. Aunt Branwell has been unfairly accused by early biographers of being a strict Calvinist and frightening the young Anne, who shared her aunt's room as a child, into a state of religious melancholy. It is often forgotten that it was she who enabled the Brontës to fulfil two of their dreams. When Charlotte longed to go to Brussels to further her education, it was Aunt Branwell, with her small private income, who funded the trip in 1842, and on her death later that year, she provided legacies for her nieces that enabled them to pay for the publication of their *Poems* in 1846, thus setting them on the path to literary success.

The children felt the loss of their mother keenly, for though they never really remembered her, her absence in their lives is reflected in the number of orphans and motherless children who feature in their early writings and novels. Maria, the eldest at just seven, to some extent took the mother's place in the younger children's affections. She was a clever and wise child with whom Mr Brontë said he could discuss the issues of the day as easily as with an adult. However, Mr Brontë found himself a widower in his mid-forties, in a moorland parish where he was unlikely to meet another suitable partner. The law dictated that a man could not marry his deceased wife's sister and so, no doubt thinking that it was unfair to keep Aunt Branwell in Haworth, he made attempts to find a wife who might be a mother to his children as well as a companion for himself. It is likely that at the close of 1821 he proposed to Elizabeth Firth, who would have been appalled at being asked just three months after Maria's death, and did not communicate with the family for another two years, though she appears to have forgiven any such lapse later. He may also have proposed to Isabella Dury, the sister of a friend. Finally Patrick wrote to Mary Burder, to whom he had been engaged in Wethersfield over fifteen years earlier, but she refused him sharply as there was some residual bitterness over their past relationship. Each woman would have found the prospect of living in Haworth with a paltry income and six small children a trial, even had they loved

Patrick deeply. Aunt Branwell remained at Haworth and Mr Brontë had to settle for the prospect of a lonely old age where romance was concerned. He turned himself to considering his children's futures.

Mr Brontë was very proud of his only son. The red-headed Branwell was lively, witty and excitable and the family all believed that a glittering career in the arts lay ahead for him. Career options for women were severely restricted. The professions were not open to them, universities did not award women degrees, and the only resort for an educated woman was teaching, being a governess or writing. Mr Brontë's five daughters had no social position or dowry to recommend them to a wealthy husband, so though keen on education for both sexes for its own sake, Mr Brontë knew that their best hope was to be well-educated, thus enabling them to earn an independent living should he die before them. In such a case, they would inherit nothing and be turned out of their home, for the Parsonage was church property and only the incumbent was allowed to live there, rent free.

Initially Mr Brontë sent his two eldest daughters, Maria and Elizabeth, to Crofton Hall School, near Wakefield, a school earlier attended by Elizabeth

Firth and Fanny Outhwaite, both godmothers to the Brontë children. They only spent a short time there, however, probably because Patrick could not afford the fees and he had three more girls to educate. The opening of the Clergy Daughters' School at Cowan Bridge, Tunstall, beyond Skipton in Yorkshire, must have seemed like the answer to his prayers. The school is notorious for being the basis of Lowood charity school in Charlotte's *Jane Eyre*. Cowan Bridge was run by the Revd William Carus Wilson, author of magazines such as *The Children's Friend* and *The Friendly Visitor*, which featured the terrible consequences for little children if they thwarted God's wishes. Mr Brocklehurst of Lowood was based on Carus Wilson. Cowan Bridge included many famous names on its list of patrons, several of whom Mr Brontë knew personally. The school espoused strict discipline, in keeping with the majority of schools in the early nineteenth century. It was designed to provide a basic education for the children of impecunious clerics, with additional instruction for the more academic girls, with a view to their becoming governesses. Maria and Elizabeth were admitted to the school in July 1824, with Charlotte joining them in August and Emily in

November. All were to be educated as governesses with the exception of Elizabeth, who had sound common sense and was probably intended to be the family housekeeper.

Mr Brontë obviously suspected nothing amiss, or he would not have sent the two younger girls to join their sisters. However, Cowan Bridge suffered from poor diet and hygiene in food preparation, encouraging the spread of disease. Maria fell ill and left school on 14 February 1825. Charlotte and Emily never saw their beloved eldest sister again. She died of tuberculosis at home on 6 May. The Cowan Bridge Register notes, 'Her father's account of her is; "she exhibited during her illness many symptoms of a heart under divine influence"'.[5] Charlotte blamed the school for her death and over twenty years later she recreated Maria in the character of the saintly Helen Burns in *Jane Eyre*. Elizabeth also fell ill and was sent home at the end of May. Deeply alarmed, Mr Brontë immediately withdrew Charlotte and Emily. The perceptive entry in the school registers on Charlotte's departure reads, 'Altogether clever of her age but knows nothing systematically'.[6] Elizabeth died of tuberculosis on 15 June and was buried beside her mother and sister in the family vault beneath Haworth church. Charlotte was now the eldest of the four surviving Brontë children and the responsibility was to weigh heavily on her all her life.

The period from 1825 to 1831, despite the terrible loss of Maria and Elizabeth, was one of the happiest for the Brontë children. They were all together, yet to face adult responsibilities, and deeply involved in a shared imaginary world that formed the springboard for their literary talents later in life.

However, when Charlotte reached thirteen, her father knew further formal education was required if his daughters were to be employable. Mr Brontë settled on Roe Head school, in Mirfield, near Huddersfield, and close to his former home at Hartshead. Charlotte, remembering the last occasion on which the family had been separated at Cowan Bridge, must have dreaded the experience, for she was to be at Roe Head alone.

THREE

ROE HEAD AND SCRIBBLEMANIA, 1831–5

During Charlotte's first days at Roe Head school in January 1831, Ellen Nussey, a fellow pupil, discovered a little, weeping, shrinking figure in the shadows of the library, a picture which is echoed in the opening chapter of *Jane Eyre* when the young Jane takes refuge among the books. With an instinctive sympathy Ellen comforted the homesick and sensitive thirteen-year-old girl. Charlotte and Ellen, the daughter of a sociable manufacturing family living at the Rydings, Birstall, quickly became friends and that friendship lasted throughout their lives. It is to Ellen that we owe the preservation of hundreds of Charlotte's letters, letters that reveal so much about the Brontë family. At Roe Head Charlotte also encountered another lifelong friend, Mary Taylor, whose family lived at the Red House, Gomersal. Mary's Radical politics conflicted with Charlotte's High Tory views and the two spent much time in furious political debate. The three friends were very different in temperament. Ellen was the more dutiful, quiet and conventional type, while Mary was forthright, independent and energetic. Each reflected two sides of Charlotte's character, Ellen the faithful friend who would supply gossip, advice on clothes, and stability; Mary the literary and political animal, who constantly surprised Charlotte and spurred her on to achieve her goals. Mary spent some time running her own business in New Zealand but continued to correspond with Charlotte and Ellen, and later in life became a published writer, producing articles on women's issues and one novel, *Miss Miles*. Unfortunately Mary destroyed almost all of Charlotte's letters to her.

Roe Head, run by Miss Margaret Wooler and her three sisters, was very unlike Cowan Bridge. It was a pleasant building, later sketched by both Charlotte and Anne, set in attractive grounds. Cowan Bridge had over fifty pupils when Charlotte and Emily were there but here there were less than a dozen girls, mostly the daughters of the nearby manufacturing families, and the routine was much more relaxed and civilized. Initially Charlotte was mortified to find herself lacking in the basic elements of grammar and geography. However, she loved to acquire knowledge for its own sake, as well as from a sense of duty to her family, and so she worked hard and quickly reached a standard of excellence that merited the award of a medal for achievement.

At this time, Ellen commented on Charlotte's Irish lilt. Mr Brontë had an Irish accent, presumably diluted a little by his years spent at Cambridge, and some of his inflections and turns of phrase probably found their way into his daughter's speech. No one else remarked upon the accents of Charlotte or her siblings subsequently, so the class-conscious Charlotte probably developed an unremarkable educated Northern accent.

The new pupil was very short-sighted and thus did not play the piano or join in with ball games, but she amazed her fellow pupils with her knowledge of literature and art, which she shared with them happily. Art education for girls was mostly limited to the copying of prints and exercises but Charlotte

benefited from having had lessons at Haworth with
a local artist, John Bradley, probably between 1829
and 1830. Many Brontë drawings from this period
survive, including sheets covered in mouths, noses
and eyes from different angles. A recently
discovered album, kept by a pupil or teacher at Roe
Head, contains poems, drawings and watercolours
by pupils, including a sketch by Charlotte.[1] To the
modern eye, the Brontës' artistic skill seems
remarkable but the Roe Head album enables us to
see that although Charlotte's and Emily's work is
better than average, it is not that far removed from
the level of accomplishment shown by most
educated young women of the period.

What was unusual about Charlotte Brontë was
her storytelling skills: Ellen recalled her friend
thrilling the dormitory to shrieking pitch with a
night-time tale of a sleepwalker. While Ellen
admired her new friend's sense of drama, and she
and Mary had been told a little of the writing she
pursued at home, they could not suspect the
depth of the obsession that Charlotte had shared
for several years with Branwell, Emily and Anne:
the Brontës' imaginary worlds of Angria and
Gondal.

From their early childhood, the Brontës had created plays and stories that they then recorded in handmade 'little books', scraps of paper sewn together, some less than two inches high. These they filled with tiny handwriting made to resemble print and laid out in mimicry of real books, with headings, contents pages and publication details. Patrick obviously knew that his children had rich imaginations, for he told Elizabeth Gaskell that he was often called in to settle some dispute arising from their play. On one occasion he inscribed a blank notebook belonging to Charlotte with the instruction that everything written in it should be in a neat and legible hand, indicating that he was fully aware of the children's private fantasies.

The childhood characters and themes developed through adolescence and into adulthood; the manuscripts by then were produced on larger sheets of paper but retained the private minuscule handwriting. The Brontës had served a literary apprenticeship of over twenty years by the time their novels were published. Their genius did not appear overnight.

Although Patrick Brontë's small income did not allow for luxuries, the Brontës nevertheless had access to newspapers and magazines and key texts of the time. Their library was limited but select and every book was studied avidly. As the children of a clergyman, they were most influenced by the Bible. Biblical knowledge was a shared cultural assumption in the nineteenth century and there are numerous Biblical and literary allusions in the Brontës' mature works. Particular favourites with all the family were the novels of Walter Scott, Shakespeare and the poetry of Lord Byron. Unusually, Mr Brontë allowed his daughters access to the complete works of Shakespeare and Byron, for it was common practice to edit out content deemed 'unsuitable' for delicate female minds. Charlotte's favourite books can be determined from her list of suggested reading for Ellen: Milton, Shakespeare, Thomson, Goldsmith, Pope, Scott, Byron, Campbell, Wordsworth and Southey. The family also enjoyed the poetry of William Cowper, Bunyan's *Pilgrim's Progress* and the Arabian Nights stories, and they all copied vignettes from Thomas Bewick's *A History of British Birds*, mentioned in the first chapter of *Jane Eyre*. Their favourite reading was the monthly *Blackwood's Edinburgh Magazine*, which included news of exploration, poetry, literary review, politics and humour.

Branwell wrote to *Blackwood's* in 1835 and 1837, begging to be allowed to present his work. Unfortunately, his correspondence was couched in naïvely arrogant terms and he never received a reply.

The four children, very close in age and with similar interests and sentiments, needed no other playmates and were isolated somewhat by being one of the few educated families in the area. They played games like any other children, and were noisy, mischievous and boisterous, once alarming their servant terribly by screaming until she thought they had all gone mad. However, their games were based on the raw materials at hand, and the incident which seems to have sparked their creativity was the arrival of a set of toy soldiers that Mr Brontë purchased for Branwell in 1826. Each child selected a soldier and named him. The soldiers became known as the 'Young Men' and later as the 'Twelves'. They travelled through Africa and founded the Glass Town Confederacy, later to become Angria. The children became the four 'Genii', who had power of life and death over the inhabitants of their imaginary world. Initially Branwell's battles and politics took precedence but Charlotte developed her interests in characterization, description and passionate romance, while Emily and Anne founded their own land of Gondal which naturally developed further when Charlotte went to Roe Head in 1831. None of Emily and Anne's prose juvenilia has survived but Charlotte's and Branwell's manuscripts are filled with humour, melodrama and improbabilities. It is difficult to determine precisely where the 'juvenilia' ends and the Brontës' mature writing begins, as Emily was still writing about Gondal in her late twenties and the majority of the poems which appeared in their collection published in 1846 are based on Angrian and Gondal themes. The spelling and grammar of the early works are often atrocious, they are sometimes repetitive and dull, but they do provide a fascinating insight into the development of the Brontës' writing style and the themes that preoccupied them throughout their writing lives.

By June 1832, Charlotte had acquired as much learning as possible and came home to pass on her knowledge to her sisters. Even a modest school like Roe Head was a drain on Mr Brontë's limited resources and educating his eldest daughter to a level where she might then instruct her sisters was sensible practice. Thus the four children were reunited and able to continue a happy programme of lessons with their father, aunt and Charlotte, interspersed with long walks on the moors and private study time where they read, talked and developed further chronicles of Angria and Gondal. This was the last such period before the necessity of earning a living imposed itself on the Brontës' close-knit lives.

Branwell had lessons in oil painting from William Robinson in the 1830s and it was around this time that he painted the now famous portrait of his three sisters.[2] This is an atmospheric image painted in about 1834 when Branwell was in his late teens. The three sisters gaze out at us through the cracked canvas, Anne with finely arched eyebrows and a long nose, Emily with an impenetrable gaze and firm lips, and Charlotte with her large forehead and short-sighted eyes. Branwell originally included himself in the composition but painted the image out. He also painted another group portrait, known as the 'gun group',[3] which, apart from the well-known, haunting profile fragment of Emily,[4] is now lost, presumed destroyed by Arthur Bell Nicholls, Charlotte's widower. Charlotte was keen to become an artist at this time and it was recently discovered[5] that she did in fact exhibit two of her pictures, pencil studies of Kirkstall Abbey and Bolton Abbey, at the Royal Northern Society for the Encouragement of the Fine Arts in Leeds in 1834. However, a successful career in art was notoriously difficult, doubly so for women, and in later life when her publishers asked her if she would consider illustrating a new edition of *Jane Eyre*, Charlotte declined.

In July 1835, Charlotte was to return to Roe Head School as a teacher. Childhood had definitely come to an end. The cushion of home life was removed and the harsh light of economic necessity forced the 'infernal world' of Angria into the darkness of a guilty obsession that was to cause Charlotte great conflict over the next few years.

FOUR

EARNING A
LIVING, 1835–45

O ne of the main themes of the Brontës' writing
is their own experience of education and the
need to earn a living. *Jane Eyre* is a passionate attack
on the class system and all of Charlotte's novels
feature teaching, education or the position of
women in some form. Similarly Anne's *Agnes Grey* is
a searingly truthful exposé of what life as a
governess was actually like, and *The Tenant of Wildfell
Hall* is a powerful condemnation of a system that
favoured the wealthy and the male sex over women
and the poor. Even *Wuthering Heights*, a novel less
obviously rooted in the issues of society, presents
education as a hopeful escape route by which the
second generation of characters rid themselves of
Heathcliff's tyranny.

In July 1835, at the age of nineteen, Charlotte
was taken on as a teacher at Roe Head, with Emily

accompanying her as a free pupil. Emily had not attended school since the few months spent at Cowan Bridge when she was barely six years old, and now her independent spirit struggled against the strictures of school life. She stayed just a few months and was replaced by Anne, who was better equipped to tolerate being away from home. Emily's experience of Roe Head was stifling. She could not adapt to the restrictions placed upon her freedom and became seriously ill with homesickness. She remained at home until September 1838, when she took a situation as a teacher at Miss Patchett's school at Law Hill, on the hillside above Halifax, but again she endured the position for only a few months. Each occasion seems to have had little impact on Emily's sense of identity, merely reinforcing her self-sufficient stubbornness.

Anne stayed at Roe Head as a pupil until December 1837 but Charlotte's time was fully occupied with teaching and their worlds seem to have been very separate, each sister battling her own personal demons. Anne became unwell with flu towards the end of 1837, an illness probably exacerbated by a profound religious crisis. A nearby Moravian minister attended her and was able to give her some comfort, emphasizing the forgiving nature of God. Charlotte was alarmed by Anne's condition and angry with herself and Miss Wooler for not noticing it earlier. She and Anne left the school.

However, Charlotte was persuaded to return to her post in 1838, though the school was now in new premises at Dewsbury Moor. Having reassured herself as to Anne's recovery, Charlotte continued to cope with her own crisis – a conflict between duty and pleasure. She had confided in Ellen that she feared she would be damned for the evil thoughts that sometimes occupied her mind. Charlotte did not reveal another reason for her dilemma. Her obsession with Angria was conflicting with her duty and the passion of her thoughts frightened her. While she was teaching, Charlotte wrote in her precious free time. The surviving fragments of what is described as her 'Roe Head Journal' are among the most startling of the Brontës' manuscripts. They are written in the minuscule handwriting common to the majority of the Brontës' private thoughts and the lines run into each other in many places: Charlotte was composing with great speed, in an almost trancelike state, sometimes with her eyes closed, as she summoned another vision from the infernal world of Angria. Most of the fragments follow a similar pattern, in which the young teacher manages to snatch a few moments of privacy to write, struggles to recreate the mood and open the channels of creativity, begins to be possessed by a story and finally the spell is broken by the arrival of a prosaic pupil with a query. Charlotte's condemnation of her pupils is total: 'just then a Dolt came up with a lesson. I thought I should have vomited.'[1]

It was this heated, almost manic tendency which Charlotte conveyed in her well-known correspondence with the poet laureate, Robert Southey, whose work she had long admired. The twenty-year-old Charlotte had sent Southey some of her poetry, asking his advice and, though he recognized her ability, he added the famous put-down, 'Literature cannot be the business of a woman's life, & it ought not to be'.[2] Such a view of women was not uncommon at the time. The rest of Southey's letter has often been ignored but Charlotte treasured his advice and, as a successful novelist, reflected that he had checked her youthful excesses, helping her to rid herself of a tendency towards idolatry and to focus her work with greater clarity. This process was developed further when she encountered her influential teacher, Constantin Heger, in Brussels several years later.

Meanwhile Branwell's education was progressing along different lines. He was instructed in the Classics by his father, lessons which, unusually for girls at the time, his sisters may have shared; Anne was to teach Latin at Thorp Green and Emily translated sections from Homer. For some time Branwell had been taking art lessons from William Robinson, a Bradford artist who had been a pupil of Sir Thomas Lawrence, and at one point it was thought that he might study at the Royal Academy. Scholars had always assumed this to be the first in a long line of failures for Branwell, that he had arrived in London but returned home under a mysterious cloud within a few days of setting out. This assumption was based on a draft letter to the Academy written in the summer of 1835 by Branwell and his juvenile manuscript featuring a character called Charles Wentworth, who is overwhelmed by his first visit to Verdopolis (London). However, a recently discovered letter, written in November 1835,[3] from Branwell and his father to William Robinson, indicates that Branwell never went to London to present his portfolio. He was advised by his tutor that, before applying to the Academy in the summer of 1836, he would need to improve his grasp of anatomy and the Classics, and at least one further course of tuition was suggested during the ensuing winter. Branwell never went to London subsequently, presumably because his talents were not rated highly enough by his tutor.

Critics of Mr Brontë have often wondered why he did not send his only son to university, enabling him to benefit from the same opportunities that he had enjoyed at Cambridge. A letter of February 1838 that came to light a few years ago reveals that Mr Brontë had considered 'the mercantile line' for his son, and then turned his attention 'to a University Education, but this would require great expense, and four or five years from hence, ere he could, in a pecuniary way, do any thing for himself'.[4] Mr Brontë simply could not afford to send Branwell away. He also made enquiries about a banking career for his son but this came to nothing and in June 1838 Branwell was set up as a portrait painter in Bradford, lodging with Mr and Mrs Isaac Kirby of 3 Fountain Street. In this way Branwell was able to meet a new circle of artists and engravers, including the sculptor Joseph Bentley Leyland and artist John Hunter Thompson. Within less than a year, Branwell returned home in debt, though probably not through any fault of his own other than lack of ability and luck. Branwell's surviving oils show that his grasp of the difficult oil painting techniques and draughtsmanship was patchy. The cost of further lessons would have been high and provincial artists of moderate ability would soon be superseded by the new art of photographic portraiture. The idea of an artistic career was shelved.

In April 1839 Anne had become governess to the Inghams of Blake Hall, Mirfield, the first of the three sisters to find a situation with a private family. Charlotte seemed surprised by her youngest sister's self-possession and independence, even though Anne was by now nineteen years old. Anne left Blake Hall in December of the same year and in May 1840 she became governess to the Robinsons of Thorp Green Hall, Little Ouseburn, near York, a situation she was to retain for five years, the most enduring of all the Brontë children's attempts to earn a living. The undisciplined little Inghams and the coquettish Robinson girls provided some inspiration for the spitting, cruel children and the portrait of Rosalie Murray in *Agnes Grey*. It was while accompanying the Robinsons on holiday to Scarborough, a spa town on the east coast of Yorkshire, that Anne first glimpsed the sea, which was to captivate her and feature in both of her novels.

In March 1839, Charlotte received an unexpected, business-like proposal of marriage from Ellen's brother, the Revd Henry Nussey. He had contemplated missionary work and the experience may have influenced Charlotte's depiction of the chilly missionary, the Revd St John Rivers, in *Jane Eyre*. For Charlotte, love was a prerequisite of marriage, though many women would have considered her foolish not to grasp the opportunity of financial security. She refused a second proposal of marriage that year from a visiting Irish curate, Mr Pryce, whom she had only met on one occasion.

In May Charlotte tried her hand as a governess, with Mr and Mrs Sidgwick of Stonegappe, Lothersdale, near Skipton, but she hated it and left in July. She found her charges impossible, the menial tasks degrading, and she hated the isolated and humiliating position of being neither family nor

servant. It would seem that she was highly unsuited
to such a position, imagining slights where none
were intended, feeling invisible if no one spoke to
her and angry if she were ordered to do something.
Branwell had a short period as a tutor to the
Postlethwaite family of Broughton-in-Furness in
Cumbria from January to June 1840. He enjoyed
the spectacular countryside of the Lake District and
its associations with poets and writers. The highlight
of his stay was when he sent examples of his work
to the poet Hartley Coleridge and was invited to
meet him. Coleridge was enthusiastic about
Branwell's translation of the first book of Horace's
Odes. The reasons for his leaving the Postlethwaites
are unclear but there is an unproven suggestion that
he may have fathered a child there, which
subsequently died.

September 1840 saw Branwell employed in a
new role, eschewing the arts and becoming a clerk
on the new Leeds to Manchester railway at Sowerby
Bridge, near Halifax. The job itself was tedious but
the railway was a new and exciting mode of
transport with prospects for young, ambitious men.
While there and in his next position from April
1841, when he was promoted to clerk-in-charge at

Luddenden Foot station, Branwell was able to meet a whole circle of artists and writers and his friend Francis Grundy. From 1841 Branwell began to see some small success in having his poetry published in the local newspapers. He was actually the first of the children to see their work in print, a fact often forgotten when early biographers portrayed Branwell as a hopeless drunk from an early age. Branwell certainly enjoyed a drink, like most young men, and his time on the railways was marked by one or two nights of heavy carousing.

Meanwhile, in March 1841, Charlotte had taken another position as a governess, this time with the Whites of Upperwood House, Rawdon, between Bradford and Leeds, but she left the same December. Turning their thoughts to another means of independence, the sisters contemplated opening their own school at the Parsonage, and Charlotte mentioned the idea to Ellen in July 1841. She knew that travel abroad would be necessary to gain additional proficiency in languages and the extra polish which would attract pupils, though in the end no pupils materialized. She itched to travel, especially as Mary and Martha Taylor were at school in Europe at the time. On 29 September Charlotte wrote to her aunt, requesting the sum of between fifty and a hundred pounds to enable her and Emily, whom she had determined would share the experience, for Anne was settled at Thorp Green, to travel abroad. Her initial idea was to go to Paris but expense determined that Brussels was more within their means.

In February 1842, Charlotte and Emily, accompanied by their father, set off for Brussels and the Pensionnat Heger where the sisters were to be students. The Brontës were marked out from the other girls by being in their mid-twenties, English, Protestant (as opposed to the dominant Catholic culture of Brussels) and somewhat provincial. The experience, while opening their horizons to European books and new ways of thinking, also seems to have served to accentuate their differences and individuality – rather than adapting to Continental ways, the sisters became more resolutely themselves, defining the voices that were to speak out so strongly in their novels. Charlotte's early writings were often overblown and overly romantic, yet she had learned how to handle dialogue, narrative, description and character. From 1839 until her published works appeared, only a small number of Charlotte's manuscripts survive. It is therefore highly likely that the Brussels experience between 1842 and 1843 was crucial to her development as a writer, teaching her to edit herself and, through the discipline of thinking in a foreign language, to focus on achieving clarity. Since none of Emily's prose juvenilia survives, it is impossible to draw any sort of a conclusion as to how Brussels may have affected her work.

The Pensionnat Heger was run by Zoe Heger and her husband, Constantin Heger, then in his early thirties, who taught there and at the nearby boys' school. Emily suffered her usual homesickness when away from Haworth but she bore it with resolve, aware that what she learned might be the means of running a school at her beloved home. The sisters concentrated on French, the elements of German and drawing, and Emily had music lessons from one of the best music professors in Belgium. Ellen recalled that Emily played with precision and brilliancy and in Brussels she taught three pupils of her own.

Constantin Heger was a charismatic and temp-eramental teacher, whom Charlotte first likened to an insane tom-cat and a delirious hyena because of

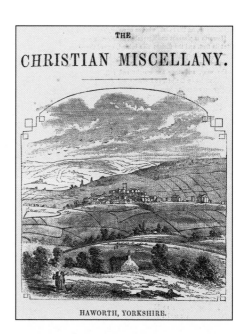

THE
CHRISTIAN MISCELLANY.

HAWORTH, YORKSHIRE.

Haworth, *c.* 1858. From *The Christian Miscellany and Family Visiter*. (The Brontë Parsonage Museum)

Haworth Parsonage, *c.* 1850–5, from an ambrotype. This was the Brontës' home from 1820 until 1861 and is now the Brontë Parsonage Museum. (The Brontë Parsonage Museum)

Portrait said to show Patrick Brontë as a young man. (The Brontë Parsonage Museum)

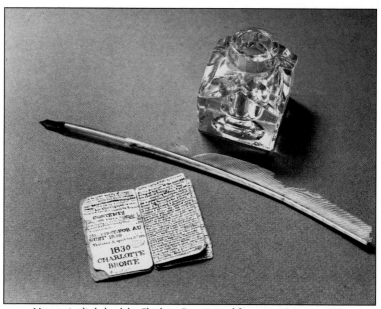

Manuscript little book by Charlotte Brontë, aged fourteen, 12 August 1830.
(The Brontë Parsonage Museum)

Pencil copy of a wood engraving by Thomas Bewick by Branwell Brontë, aged eleven,
2 June 1829. (The Brontë Parsonage Museum)

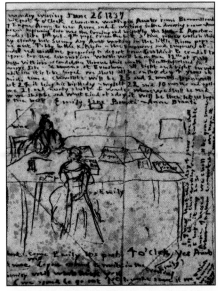

Emily Brontë's diary paper, 26 June 1837. Emily and Anne recorded details of family life and their imaginary world of Gondal in an irregular series of 'diary papers'. This sketch shows the two sisters writing. (The Brontë Parsonage Museum)

This sketch by Branwell Brontë shows him being summoned from sleep by the figure of Death. It is one of his last surviving drawings. (The Brontë Parsonage Museum)

A manuscript fragment written when Charlotte Brontë was a teacher at Roe Head School, 1836. (The Brontë Parsonage Museum)

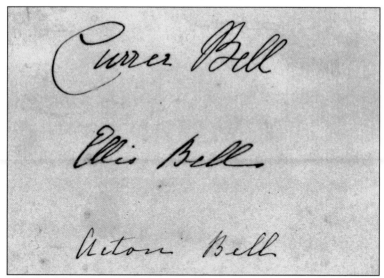

The Brontës' pseudonyms. The signatures of Currer, Ellis and Acton Bell, 23 July 1846.
(The Brontë Parsonage Museum)

A poster for an early stage production of *Jane Eyre*, the Globe Theatre, Boston, 1875. *Jane Eyre* was first dramatized just five months after the novel was published. (The Brontë Parsonage Museum)

"You have saved my life — I have a pleasure in owing you so immense a Debt — I cannot say more — nothing else that had being life would have been tolerable to me in the character of creditor for such an obligation — but you — it is different — I feel your benefits no burden — Jane—" he paused — gazed at me — words almost visible, trembled on his lips — but his voice was checked —

"Good-night again, sir — there is no debt, benefit, burden, obligation in the case —"

"I knew" he continued "you would do me good in some way, at some time; I saw it in your eyes when I first beheld you — their expression and smile did not — (again he stopped) did not (he proceeded, hastily) strike delight to my very inmost heart so for nothing — People talk of natural sympathies; I have heard of good genii; there are grains of truth in the wildest Fable — my cherished Preserver, good-night —!"

Strange energy was in his voice, strange fire in his eyes look—

"I am glad I happened to be awake." I said, and then I was going.

"What — you will go?"

"I am cold, sir."

"Cold? yes — and standing in a pool! Go then, Jane, go!" But he still retained my hand, and I could not free it; I bethought myself of an expedient.

"I think I hear Mrs Fairfax move, sir." said I.

From Charlotte's manuscript of *Jane Eyre*, 'You have saved my life – I have a pleasure of owing you so immense a debt . . .'. (The British Library, Add. 43474, folio 154)

Milton Rosmer as Heathcliff and Ann Trevor as Cathy from the 1920 silent film version of *Wuthering Heights*, the first known dramatization of the novel. (The Brontë Parsonage Museum)

his melodramatic enthusiasm. However he was also disciplined, kind and inspirational, leaving a deep impression on all of his pupils. A key to his teaching method was emulation: he would encourage his pupils to study the methods by which authors achieved their effects, then try to reproduce those effects in their own writing, always directing the piece to the point, yet allowing room for self-expression. He emphasized the importance of acquiring technique before one could produce art, something that Branwell had struggled to achieve in his painting. Heger's encouragement of individuality meant that the lines between teacher and friend sometimes became blurred. A study of Charlotte's and Emily's surviving French essays (*devoirs*) shows that Emily had already developed a disciplined and logical way of thinking, and she often found herself challenging Heger's judgement. Charlotte required more personal attention, which she was to misinterpret.

Back in Haworth, Branwell's period at Luddenden Foot had come to an end when he was dismissed for being negligent in keeping the accounts. It was not suggested that he had stolen money himself, but that he had failed to keep proper records which would subsequently have drawn attention to the dishonesty of his assistant. On 6 September 1842 William Weightman died. He had come to Haworth as Mr Brontë's curate in August 1839 and had enlivened the Parsonage with his charm and good humour. It is often believed that Anne was in love with Weightman but there is little evidence of this. He and Branwell had maintained a close friendship, and Branwell was distraught by his friend's death from cholera at the age of twenty-six. This tragedy was swiftly followed by the illness and death of Aunt Branwell on 29 October. Branwell, the only member of the family at home at this time apart from his father, found nursing the aunt whom he had regarded as a mother a terrible strain, especially after the deaths of his own mother and his beloved eldest sister Maria.

Charlotte and Emily came home immediately on notification of their aunt's death. In January 1843 Anne returned to Thorp Green, taking Branwell with her as tutor to the young Edmund Robinson. Emily remained at home thankfully, acting as housekeeper in her aunt's place and free to organize her time as she wished. She now had the assistance of Martha Brown, the sexton John Brown's young daughter, who had started to help the elderly Tabby in 1840. Charlotte returned to Brussels.

By the spring of 1843, Zoe Heger was subtly restricting the contact between the young Englishwoman and her husband, for she had noticed what Charlotte could not admit to herself, that the deep admiration she felt for Heger was in danger of developing into something more. Heger himself seems to have been unaware of this but the lonely Charlotte, always given to forming strong attachments, clung to his every word. Charlotte was to portray Zoe Heger as the sneaky Madame Beck in her novel *Villette* (1853) and her husband as Monsieur Paul Emanuel. When Charlotte returned from Brussels for the last time, she spent the next year in a state of misery, pining for Heger. Four letters from Charlotte to Heger, dated 24 July and 24 October 1844 and 8 January and 18 November 1845, survive in the British Library. Heger tore them up but they were rescued by his wife from the wastepaper basket and taped or stitched together again. Charlotte does not go so far as to declare her love for Heger but she implores him to contact her as a letter would be food and drink to her. It is interesting that she addresses him as her 'master' on several occasions, a term which Jane Eyre uses to describe the moody Rochester. He did not reply and Charlotte assigned the bitter events to experience. She could not discuss her feelings with Emily and there was little excitement in the village to distract her. But, in May 1845, a new curate arrived in Haworth. Arthur Bell Nicholls, a dark-haired young Irishman, appears to have attracted no interest from Charlotte at this stage and indeed she scolded Ellen for speculating on Haworth gossip that he and she were romantically involved. Nine years later they were to be married.

During the previous ten years the Brontës had hardly been at home together. Their shared routine of writing had been interrupted by the necessity of earning a living away from home, and each had developed their own methods of working and their own distinctive styles. As Charlotte chafed at home, she can little have suspected the drama that was unfolding at Thorp Green.

FIVE

DISGRACE AND DETERMINATION, 1845–7

When Branwell joined Anne at Thorp Green in 1843 as tutor to the Robinsons' young son, Edmund, he quickly became valued in his situation. He was well educated, lively and by all accounts a charming conversationalist. However, the whole experience was to end two years later in disgrace for Branwell, precipitating a downward spiral of despair, ill health and dependency on alcohol and drugs. His predicament placed tremendous strain on his family and increased the necessity for his sisters to find a means of earning a living.

Anne resigned from her position as governess at Thorp Green, probably unable to tolerate the situation any longer, and returned home in June 1845. She was accompanied by Branwell, who then moved on to the coast. At this stage the rest of the family were unaware of Branwell's problems. Emily and Anne decided to take their first long journey together and travelled by train to York, staying there overnight. Even at the age of nearly twenty-seven, Emily was still happily involved in the imaginary world of Gondal. In her diary paper of July 1845[1] Emily described how the two young women acted out various roles on their journey, 'escaping from the Palaces of Instruction to join the Royalists who are hard driven at present by the victorious Republicans . . . the Gondals still flourish as bright as ever'. Anne, by contrast, noted in her diary paper that the Gondals were in a sad state. She was depressed, for during her time at Thorp Green she had witnessed what she described as 'some very unpleasant and undreamt of experience of human nature', her brother's immoral relationship with a married woman.[2]

Once Emily and Anne returned from their visit to York, Charlotte went to visit Ellen, who was staying with her brother Henry at Hathersage in Derbyshire. A result of this visit was a tangible piece of inspiration for one of the most Gothic scenes in *Jane Eyre*. At Hathersage Charlotte visited North

Lees Hall, home of the Eyre family, whose furnishings included a large carved cupboard[3] which, like that in Chapter 20 of *Jane Eyre*, was decorated with portraits of the twelve Apostles in 'grim design'.[4] In the novel it stands in the shadowy, tapestried room on the third floor, the faces of the apostles watching as Jane nurses the terrified and bloodied Mason, while the madwoman who attacked him occupies the chamber next door.

When Charlotte returned to Haworth on 26 July, she found Branwell ill and next to madness. He had been dismissed by Mr Robinson for 'proceedings bad beyond expression'[5] and was theatened with exposure if he attempted to comunicate with any member of the Robinson family. Branwell claimed that he had had an affair with Mrs Lydia Robinson, his employer's wife, an attractive woman seventeen years his senior. The extent of their relationship has long been a subject of debate but the full text of Branwell's letter to his friend Francis Grundy[6] came to light recently and it implies that the love affair not only existed but was physical. Branwell wrote, 'During nearly three years I had daily "troubled pleasure soon chastised by fear" in the society of one whom I must, till death, call my <u>wife</u>', and he referred to Mr Robinson as a 'eunuch-like fellow who though possessed of such a treasure never even occupied the same apartment with her . . .'. Additionally Branwell fully believed that they would marry if her husband died. However a woman like Lydia Robinson may have been flattered by the attentions of a younger man but would not have sacrificed her social position to marry a penniless tutor.

Charlotte believed Lydia Robinson to be a scheming woman who had toyed with her brother's affections and then dropped him when her adultery was discovered. Branwell continued to receive news and sums of money from Thorp Green via intermediaries such as the Robinsons' family doctor, though he was not told the truth. It is highly unlikely that the worldly Lydia Robinson was pining away for the love of her son's tutor and contemplating entering a nunnery. Equally no clause has been found in her husband's will to disinherit her if she recommenced her relationship with Branwell, though the latter obviously believed it at the time, writing to Leyland, 'I have got my finishing stroke at last and I feel stunned to marble by the blow'.[7]

Gaskell's portrayal of Mrs Robinson in the *Life* in 1857 prompted legal action from her solicitors.

Though she was not named, Lydia Robinson was clearly identifiable and copies of the first edition of the biography were withdrawn and a revised edition issued.

Branwell was taken to Liverpool for a time in July 1845 by his old friend John Brown, in the hope that a change of scene would improve his health and mental state. However, he wrote to Leyland on 4 August that wherever he went, 'a certain woman robed in black and calling herself "MISERY" walked by my side, and leant on my arm as affectionately as if she were my legal wife'.[8] For the next three years until his early death in September 1848, Branwell alternated between efforts to rally his spirits enough to write and illness exacerbated by overindulgence in alcohol. He longed to be actively employed but found it difficult to keep up any sustained effort. The sketches he sent to Leyland during this period are liberally laced with macabre gravestones and images of himself being hanged or burning at the stake. His last known drawing features a self-portrait, being summoned from sleep by a skeletal figure representing Death.[9] His final published poem was 'The End of All', which appeared in the *Halifax Guardian* of 5 June 1847. It was a reworking of a poem written ten years earlier, its theme – the death of his hero Northangerland's wife – reflecting his own sense of 'bereavement' at the loss of Lydia Robinson.

While Branwell now became a cause of great concern to his family, the ever-present problem of money demanded a solution. The three sisters were together again and probably had not realised how their writing had progressed. Charlotte described how 'One day, in the autumn of 1845, I accidentally lighted on a MS volume of verse in my sister Emily's handwriting . . . something more than surprise seized me – a deep conviction that these were not common effusions, nor at all like the poetry women generally write. I thought them condensed and terse, vigorous and genuine. To my ear they also had a peculiar music – wild, melancholy, and elevating.'[10] After defusing Emily's anger at this invasion of her privacy, Charlotte persuaded her that the poems should be published and the three sisters began to select and edit their work for the press, removing references to Angrian and Gondal themes, as the majority of the poems dated from several years earlier. Charlotte explained the decision to use assumed names: 'Averse to personal publicity, we veiled our own names under those of Currer, Ellis, and Acton Bell; the ambiguous choice being dictated by a sort of conscientious scruple at assuming Christian names positively masculine, while we did not like to declare ourselves women, because – without at that time suspecting that our mode of writing and thinking was not what is called "feminine" – we had a vague impression that authoresses are liable to be looked upon with prejudice . . .'.[11]

In January 1846 the services of Aylott & Jones of London were secured by Charlotte to publish the Bells' poems. However the sisters had to pay for publication and advertising, a cost of over thirty pounds, which was funded by Aunt Branwell's legacy to her nieces. *Poems* by Currer, Ellis and Acton Bell appeared in May 1846 but as the work of unknown authors it excited little interest and sold a paltry two copies. However the collection was reviewed sparsely but well. *The Critic* of 4 July 1846 stated, 'it is long since we have enjoyed such a genuine volume of poetry as this',[12] and the *Athenaeum* of the same date was perceptive in its appreciation of Ellis's 'fine quaint spirit . . . an evident power of wing that may reach heights not here attempted'.[13] Charlotte admitted that her talents did not lie in poetry and her contribution is primarily of interest as the work of the author of *Jane Eyre*. 'The Teacher's Monologue' was written at Roe Head in 1837 and echoes her feelings of frustration and the fear of spending the rest of her life chained to teaching. Emily's poetry is of a different order altogether and had she never written *Wuthering Heights* she would still be ranked among the finest poets in the English language. Her work has been compared with that of William Blake and Emily Dickinson. It is sparse and powerful, cherishing liberty and revealing a faith in a transcendent power – a God of Nature rather than a conventional God. However, since none of Emily's Gondal prose has survived for comparison, it is difficult to judge where Gondal ends and personal poetry begins. Her poems explore themes of revenge, passionate love, exile and imprisonment, all of which resurface in *Wuthering Heights*. Anne's poetry, like her novels, uses deceptively simple ideas and expresses a quiet Christianity tempered with forceful truths. In the wake of the success of *Jane Eyre*, Smith, Elder & Co., Charlotte's second publisher, were to purchase the unsold copies of *Poems* from Aylott & Jones and reissue them with a new title page and binding in 1848.

Realizing that poetry did not sell, and that novels were more popular, the three sisters had been working on a series of tales for some time – *The Professor* by Charlotte, and *Wuthering Heights* and *Agnes Grey* – and began sending the increasingly battered parcel of manuscripts round to a succession of publishers, all of whom rejected the novels. It is interesting to note that around the same time that his sisters lit upon the idea of publishing their poems, Branwell, too, was trying to turn his talents to practical use. The previous year, in September 1845, he had written to Leyland[14] saying that he had completed one volume of a three volume novel to while away his torment: 'I knew that in the present state of the publishing and reading world a Novel is the most saleable article . . .'. It would seem that Branwell never completed his novel but his actions may have had some influence on his sisters, and vice versa, if each knew that the others were engaged in some major writing project.

Jane Eyre was begun while Charlotte lodged with her father in Manchester in August 1846. He was recovering from a cataract operation and, as he lay in a darkened room, Charlotte began the tale that was soon to grip the country.

By mid-1847 the publisher Thomas Cautley Newby of London had agreed to publish *Wuthering Heights* and *Agnes Grey* together as a two-volume set, though on terms that left Emily and Anne somewhat impoverished. They paid fifty pounds to see their books in print, with an unfulfilled promise that the money would be refunded as the books were sold. Newby apparently agreed to produce 350 copies, though Charlotte claimed that just 250 were printed. While Newby dragged his heels, *The Professor* reached the offices of Smith, Elder & Company of Cornhill, London. Although they declined to publish it, they sent the unknown author a courteous two-page letter discussing its merits and defects and saying that they would be happy to look at any other manuscript in the future. Charlotte had by now almost completed *Jane Eyre* and was delighted by this encouragement. When she dispatched the manuscript to Smith, Elder & Company on 24 August 1847, she could hardly have dared hope that it would be such a resounding popular success. Literary fame beckoned for the Brontës, but the shadow of death was not far behind.

SIX

LITERARY
SUCCESS, 1847–8

When William Smith Williams of Smith, Elder & Company read the manuscript of *Jane Eyre* he realized that the book was startlingly original. Immediately he passed it to the head of the firm, George Smith, then just twenty-four years old and a long way from his subsequent success as the greatest of the Victorian publishers. George began reading on Sunday morning and was quickly captivated by the story. He cancelled his lunchtime appointment, sent out for wine and sandwiches, ate a hasty dinner and finished the manuscript before bed that night.

On receipt of the letter from Smith, Elder & Co. saying that they were going to publish *Jane Eyre*, Charlotte was delighted. Her sisters' novels had already been accepted for publication but as yet nothing had appeared. However, Charlotte showed surprising business acumen and confidence in her work when Smith, naturally cautious with a new and unproven author, offered her just one hundred pounds for the copyright. She eventually earned around five hundred pounds for each of her novels. In contrast to Newby's slow progress, Charlotte's publishers turned her novel around with speed and professionalism. Charlotte was soon checking proofs and corresponding with London. Just six weeks after she had dispatched the manuscript, on 19 October 1847, the book appeared in three volumes, bound in claret cloth.

The reaction of critics and public was instant acclaim. What made *Jane Eyre* stand out from other novels was its freshness and outspoken views on the roles of men and women and the injustices of religion and society. The *Atlas* of 23 October commented, 'This is not merely a work of great promise; it is one of absolute performance. It is one of the most powerful domestic romances which have been published for many years. It has little or nothing of the old conventional stamp upon it; none of the jaded, exhausted attributes of a worn-out vein of imagination, reproducing old incidents . . . it is a tale of passion, not of intensity which is almost sublime.'[1] The *Examiner* pointed out that the style was 'rude and uncultivated here and there',[2] while the *Era* praised *Jane Eyre*'s 'power of thought and expression', and found it 'true, bold, well-defined and full of life – struck off by an artist who embodies his imaginings in a touch'.[3] *The People's Journal* had taken note of the 1846 edition of *Poems* and found that *Jane Eyre* was characterized by 'stern, fierce, daring dashes at portraiture – anon in subtle, startling mental anatomy – here in a grand allusion, there in an original metaphor – again in a wild gush of genuine poetry'.[4] G.H. Lewes wrote in *Fraser's Magazine* that the novel exhibited 'remarkable power' but tempered his praise by observing that there was 'too much melodrama and improbability, which smack of the circulating library'.[5] This last criticism was to affect Charlotte's approach to her next novel, *Shirley*, which she intended should be as solid and unromantic as a Monday morning.

Initial reviews of *Jane Eyre* were generally positive but after the publication of *Wuthering Heights* in December 1847 and *The Tenant of Wildfell Hall* in 1848, the accumulated uncompromising nature of the Bells' fiction proved too much for some critics. Elizabeth Rigby wrote a withering attack on *Jane Eyre*'s morality in the *Quarterly Review* of December 1848:

Whoever it be, it is a person who, with great mental powers, combines a total ignorance of the habits of society, a great coarseness of taste, and a heathenish doctrine of religion. . . . We do not hesitate to say that the tone of the mind and thought which has overthrown authority and violated every code human and divine abroad, and fostered Chartism and rebellion at home, is the same which has also written *Jane Eyre*.[6]

Meanwhile, Charlotte complained that Newby was difficult to hurry up to the proper speed and her sisters' novels were still languishing in the presses. However, Newby realized that he might be able to cash in on the success of *Jane Eyre* and so *Wuthering Heights* and *Agnes Grey* finally appeared in a three-volume set in mid-December 1847. Critical attention was mostly directed to *Wuthering Heights*, the longer work, and *Agnes Grey* was virtually ignored. Both novels were compared with *Jane Eyre* and found wanting and there was some confusion over whether the books might be the earlier work of Currer Bell. Had *Wuthering Heights* been published before *Jane Eyre*, it would have been interesting to see the critics' responses. The most common reaction to *Wuthering Heights* was repulsion and puzzlement.

The *Athenaeum* noted *Wuthering Heights'* 'power and cleverness' but shrank from its 'painful and exceptional subjects',[7] while the *Examiner* also recognized the author's 'considerable power' but found the whole novel 'wild, confused, disjointed, and improbable'.[8] Similarly the *Britannia* found the characters 'so new, so wildly grotesque, so entirely without art, that they strike us as proceeding from a mind of limited experience, but of original energy, and of a singular and distinctive cast'.[9]

One of the most tantalizing mysteries in English literature is whether Emily Brontë was working on a second novel before she died. Certainly, by the early part of 1848, Charlotte had begun to write the novel that would become *Shirley* and Anne had made considerable progress with *The Tenant of Wildfell Hall*, so it seems unlikely that Emily would not have been writing something. Emily's portable writing desk survives at the Brontë Parsonage Museum and among its contents is a letter[10] from Emily's publisher T.C. Newby, addressed simply to 'Dear Sir'. Since Emily and Anne shared the same publisher, there is a possibility that the letter may have been intended for Anne but had become detached from its envelope. When folded, the letter, dated 15 February

1848, fits precisely into the accompanying envelope, addressed to 'Ellis Bell Esq'. Newby was obviously replying to an enquiry about whether he would be prepared to accept the author's next novel, stating that he would be happy to handle it. If the letter was intended for Ellis Bell, then what happened to the presumably unfinished manuscript? It has been suggested that Charlotte found the novel after Emily's death, considered the subject matter unsuitable and destroyed it to protect her sister's reputation. The mystery extends to Emily and Anne's prose juvenilia, none of which has survived. Emily was still writing Gondal poems in the last years of her life and it is possible that she may have chosen to destroy selected elements of her own work once she realized that she was ill, in order to maintain her highly prized privacy. Emily was appalled that when Charlotte and Anne visited Smith, Elder & Co. they had let slip that they were 'three sisters', and forbade Charlotte to use her name in any correspondence. However Juliet Barker in *The Brontës* argues that Emily was unaware that she was gravely ill and probably did not have time to destroy large quantities of manuscript material. It seems unlikely that we will ever know for sure, so the debate continues.

Anne's second novel, *The Tenant of Wildfell Hall*, was published by Newby in late June 1848. It attracted instant condemnation from the critics for its foul language and scenes of debauchery, its violent hero, Gilbert Markham, and its unconventional heroine, Helen Huntingdon. The book was also criticized for its narrative structure, the large section in the middle of the book comprising Helen's diary leading some readers to lose interest in the initial sections of the novel.

On 7 July 1848 the sisters were disturbed by a letter from Smith, Elder & Co. demanding an explanation. Apparently Newby had been suggesting that Currer Bell was also the author of Ellis and Acton's novels. Acting on impulse, Charlotte and Anne decided to travel to London overnight and confront their publishers with visual evidence that there were at least two of them. Charlotte has left a lively account of this trip in a letter to Mary Taylor,[11] who had been admitted into the secret of the sisters' authorship. Emily refused to have any part in the plan and remained at home. After checking in at the Chapter Coffee House, where Charlotte had stayed *en route* to Brussels several years earlier, she and Anne proceeded to Cornhill and located the offices of Smith, Elder & Co. George Smith was called from his office and encountered two small, quietly dressed women. Charlotte placed a letter addressed to Currer Bell in his hand. Light dawned, William Smith Williams was called in, Newby was criticized on all fronts as a scoundrel and great excitement ensued. George Smith was keen to introduce his new discoveries to everyone but the sisters persuaded him against this. During their brief stay, Charlotte and Anne were taken to the opera, Charlotte acutely aware that they had not brought, nor indeed owned, any garments suitable for such an occasion, and of the odd contrast she must have made with the handsome George Smith as he led her up the staircase of the theatre. Charlotte was physically and mentally exhausted by the stress of the trip but Anne bore it with her usual quiet strength.

Soon afterwards, on 22 July, Anne wrote a Preface to the second edition of *The Tenant of Wildfell Hall*, in which she defended her book against criticisms that it was unnecessarily coarse: 'I wished to tell the truth, for truth always conveys its own moral to those who are able to receive it . . . when we have to do with vice and vicious characters, I maintain it is better to depict them as they really are than as they would wish to appear.'[12]

Branwell was in a sorry state by this time. He was drinking heavily and dependent on money given to him by his father and occasional funds passed on to him by agents of Lydia Robinson. The depths to which he had sunk are shown vividly in an undated note to John Brown from this period.[13] The handwriting is shaky, the note urgent, requesting his old friend John to obtain for him fivepence worth of gin 'in proper measure', for which he would pay him from a shilling given to him that day.

One wonders whether Branwell may have suspected that his sisters were published authors, and whether the knowledge that they had chosen to exclude him from their plans added to his misery. He, once the shining light of the family on whom all expectations were centred, had failed and it was the women who had succeeded. Since the sisters had begun working on their *Poems*, there had been a great deal of correspondence and activity at the Parsonage that would have been difficult to conceal in such a small house. After Branwell's death, Charlotte told Williams quite categorically that, 'My unhappy brother never knew that his sisters had written a line. Now he will <u>never</u> know.'[14] Did Charlotte genuinely believe this? Or did she prefer to believe it? There had been occasions where letters and packages had been opened prior to Charlotte receiving them and she wrote to Smith, Elder & Co., requesting that in future they address all correspondence to Currer Bell under cover to Miss C. Brontë to avoid confusion. It is not improbable that Branwell may have received packages accidentally, or seen reviews, proofs and copies of the Bells' novels about the house, even though he was unwell much of the time.

Apart from worries about their father's health and the inevitable disruptions caused by Branwell's behaviour, the three sisters must have looked towards the future with optimism. The literary world was speculating about the identities of the Bells and each had received praise, criticism and publicity for their work. Financial security and that rarity for women, independence, must have seemed a real possibility, and it had been achieved by doing something they loved. In the late summer of 1848 none of them could have imagined the tragedies that were to follow.

SEVEN

DARK MONTHS, 1848–9

Though generally of a robust constitution, Branwell had been ill intermittently ever since his dismissal from Thorp Green in 1845. However neither his doctor nor the family appear to have realized that his mental anguish at the loss of Lydia Robinson, and his excessive use of alcohol and opium at the end of his life, masked the symptoms of what was most likely tuberculosis. Branwell began to suffer from fainting fits and delirium tremens and was reduced to sharing his father's bedroom so that Mr Brontë could keep an eye on his son. Branwell was still sending samples of his work to his friend J.B. Leyland as late as January 1848, but further illness intervened and by the summer Branwell was seriously in debt. He had received a demand for the settlement of a bill owed to Mr Nicholson of the Old Cock inn at Halifax, 'under penalty of a court summons',[1] and was forced to request an advance of money from Dr Crosby, Lydia Robinson's agent. Branwell confessed to Leyland that if Nicholson did not wait for the money to come through and pressed him with the law 'I am RUINED. I have had five months of such utter sleeplessness, violent cough and frightful agony of mind that jail would destroy me for ever.'[2]

By now Charlotte had lost all sympathy with her childhood companion's plight, feeling that he had let the family down. Additionally Branwell's situation was not too far removed from her own. They had both cared deeply for someone older and married but Charlotte's feelings for Heger had remained frustrated and largely unspoken. Branwell had experienced at least some reciprocation of his love, if only to have his hopes cruelly dashed. Therefore it would not be surprising if she felt the need to distance herself from acknowledging the similarity of their situations.

Late in September Francis Grundy came to Haworth to invite Branwell for a meal at the Black Bull. He was appalled by the change in his friend's appearance and manner, even though he had been warned by Mr Brontë. Grundy recalled that, 'the door opened cautiously, and a head appeared. It was a mass of red, unkempt, uncut hair, wildly floating round a great, gaunt forehead; the cheeks yellow and hollow, the mouth fallen, the thin white lips not trembling but shaking, the sunken eyes, once small, now glaring with the light of madness, – all told the tale but too surely.'[3] Grundy went on to describe how Branwell rallied a little in his company, but said that his decline was the result of his relationship with Lydia Robinson and that he would welcome death. In his overwrought state, Branwell had believed that the invitation from Grundy was from the Devil and he had come to the Black Bull armed with a knife, with the intention of killing the occupant of the room.

Branwell Brontë was up and about in the village until just two days before his death on 24 September. When he was suddenly confined to his bed, the doctor was called and delivered the shocking news that Branwell had very little time to live. His family were distraught and there must have been strong feelings of guilt that his sufferings had been real physical illness, not solely selfish affectation or overindulgence. As the realization that he was dying hit home, Branwell listened to his father's pleas that he turn to God for forgiveness and his last days appear to have been calmer. John Brown came to visit his old friend and later remembered that he expressed deep affection for his family and shame at his past behaviour, whispering, 'In all my past life I have done nothing either great or good'.[4]

Branwell died on the morning of Sunday 24 September 1848, with his family beside his bed. He was just thirty-one. He was heard praying softly in his dying moments and then fell into his father's arms. Patrick cried out, 'My Son! my Son!', 'like David for Absalom',[5] Charlotte reflected. Emily and Anne's reactions are not recorded but Charlotte was ill for a week and it was left to Anne, ever strong in a crisis, to deal with her correspondence. Charlotte wrote to William Smith Williams the week after Branwell's death, describing the tragedy as a 'mercy' rather than a punishment, and saying that she wept not for the loss of her brother's companionship but for 'the wreck of talent, the ruin of promise, the untimely dreary extinction of what might have been a burning and a shining light'.[6] She said that in his death she was able to forgive him his mistakes and the pain he had caused his family, yet she still found it very hard to grieve for him without anger at his obscure end.

For some time after the funeral, Charlotte was too immersed in self-pity to notice that what appeared to be family coughs and colds masked something more serious. Emily was also unwell, having most likely contracted tuberculosis from her brother or from someone in the village. At the end of October and throughout November Charlotte was acutely concerned for her sister's health and deeply frustrated that Emily found questions about her health annoying, would accept no help of any kind, and refused to see a doctor: 'not one of her ordinary avocations will she voluntarily renounce: you must look on, and see her do what she is unfit to do, and not dare to say a word; a painful necessity for those to whom her health and existence are as precious as the life in their veins.'[7]

George Smith and William Smith Williams suggested that Charlotte send a note of Emily's symptoms to Dr Epps, an eminent homoeopathic specialist, but Emily rejected his advice as just another form of quackery. As Emily grew steadily thinner and paler, and coughed more deeply, her father, remembering the deaths of Maria and Elizabeth, realised what the outcome would be, but Charlotte still clung to an ever-decreasing hope that her sister might be spared.

The family were caught in a nightmare. Having barely come to terms with Branwell's sudden death, they now faced the possibility that Emily might die. Apart from her health, nothing mattered. Charlotte read some of the recent reviews of *Jane Eyre* and *Wuthering Heights* to her sisters around their melancholy fireside and though she tried to laugh away the criticisms, they must have hurt deeply. The publication of Anne's second novel had reopened the field for critics to attack *Jane Eyre* and *Wuthering Heights* and all three novels were branded profane, gross, revolting and animalistic. These harsh words must have rankled with Charlotte, who sprang to her sisters' defence after their deaths, attempting to absolve them of the responsibility for their unpalatable creations.

Anne continued to hear from her former pupils, Lydia Robinson's daughters Elizabeth and Mary. The Robinson girls were very fond of their former governess and visited Anne at Haworth early in December. It would seem that in the face of their mother's example, they unconsciously clung to Anne as a moral guide. On 8 November, just a few weeks after Branwell's death, the former Mrs Robinson had married Sir Edward Scott, whose first wife had died not long before. It is unlikely that she knew or cared about the fate of her son's former tutor.

Meanwhile, Emily was dangerously ill and still refusing any aid. Her stubbornness is not attractive, causing as it did great distress to her family, and one wonders what she was trying to prove. Emily is usually portrayed as mystical and sphinx-like, enigmatic and unfathomable. She was certainly all of these things but she was also stubborn to the point of stupidity. Emily insisted on continuing to carry out her household duties and to feed the dogs, Keeper and Flossy. Charlotte recalled her sister's last days:

> She made haste to leave us. Yet, while physically she perished, mentally, she grew stronger than we had yet known her. Day by day, when I saw with what a front she met suffering, I looked on her with an anguish of wonder and love. I have seen nothing like it; but, indeed, I have never seen her parallel in anything. Stronger than a man, simpler than a child, her nature stood alone.[8]

On the morning of 19 December 1848 Emily rose as usual, dressed herself and came downstairs. Her suffering was painful to watch and Charlotte wrote to Ellen, 'Moments so dark as these I have never known . . .',[9] little suspecting that Emily would die that very day. In the afternoon, Emily's condition worsened and at last she asked for a doctor to be summoned. It was too late. Emily Brontë died at two o'clock in the afternoon, aged thirty.

At the funeral Mr Brontë and Emily's faithful dog, Keeper, walked side by side behind the coffin and Keeper lay at the family's feet in the pew throughout the service, followed the coffin to the vault and then howled pitifully for days outside Emily's bedroom door. However the family's grief had to be kept in check, for their concern for Emily had masked the severity of Anne's symptoms: she was suffering from consumption. Charlotte and Mr Brontë could hardly bear to contemplate that it could happen a third time. Fearing that the local doctor would be unable to help, a specialist from Leeds came to see Anne on 5 January 1849. Ellen, who had come to stay in December to give the broken family some support, recalled his verdict.

'Mr Brontë joined us after Dr Teale's departure and, seating himself on the couch, he drew Anne towards him and said, "My *dear* little Anne". That was all — but it was understood.'[10]

To her family, Anne was brave and optimistic, taking her medicine and listening to all the advice she was given. It was felt that the consumption might be slowed if Anne rested and had a change of air in the spring. Beneath the surface Anne, approaching her twenty-ninth birthday, was frightened and angry. She had seen how the disease affected her brother and sister, she had witnessed their deaths, and the religious doubts that had haunted her in the past returned with a vengeance. On 9 January Anne began a poem that expressed her feelings at the prospect of her own death:

> A dreadful darkness closes in
> On my bewildered mind
> O let me suffer & not sin
> Be tortured yet resigned[11]

She continued the poem bitterly in the fifth and sixth verses:

> I hoped amid the brave & strong
> My portioned task might lie
> To toil amid the labouring throng
> With purpose Keen & high
>
> But thou hast fixed another part
> And thou hast fixed it well
> I said so with my bleeding heart
> When first the anguish fell[12]

Anne completed the poem at the end of the month, having come to terms with her fate. When Charlotte came to edit some of her sisters' poems in 1850, she omitted six verses in order to make Anne seem more resigned to an early death, effectively editing her sister's life to protect her memory and make her more acceptable to the public. She also suppressed further publications of *The Tenant of Wildfell Hall* after Anne's death, believing the subject matter to be a complete mistake, thus condemning the novel to years of obscurity.

Anne enjoyed a brief period of improvement in February and Charlotte again began to contemplate her own literary career, which had ground to a halt in September. Unable to be creative, she copied out the first volume of her new novel, *Shirley*, and sent it to

Smith, Elder & Co. for their opinion. Given the delicate circumstances of Charlotte's home life, of which they were fully aware from her letters, her publishers sympathetically confined themselves to generally favourable comments. However, by March, Anne was much worse. Ellen offered to have her stay to relieve the pressure on the Parsonage a little but Anne felt that it would be unfair. Unlike Emily, Anne was keen to try every possible cure. The sea air was well known as a restorative in such cases and she longed to go to her beloved Scarborough. However, in the early months of the year, Charlotte was uncertain whether the strains of the trip might outweigh the benefits. Anne wrote to Ellen Nussey to enlist her help, anxious that the sea cure should be tried in time:

> I wish it would please God to spare me not only for Papa's and Charlotte's sakes, but because I long to do some good in the world before I leave it. I have many schemes in my head for future practise – humble and limited indeed – but still I should not like them all to come to nothing, and myself to have lived to so little purpose. But God's will be done. [13]

After several delays, mostly due to Charlotte being terrified that the journey would prove too much for the invalid, Ellen came to Haworth so that the three women might travel together to York and then on to Scarborough. With what feelings the 72-year-old Patrick Brontë said goodbye to his fragile youngest daughter we can only imagine. Charlotte, Anne and Ellen arrived in Scarborough on 25 May, staying at Wood's Lodgings, No. 2, The Cliff, overlooking the sea. Anne was a model patient and found strength to enjoy the sights of Scarborough – but it was all in vain. After witnessing a wonderful sunset the previous evening, Anne died quietly and calmly at two o'clock in the afternoon on Monday 28 May 1849, on the sofa at their lodgings. Seeing how Charlotte could barely control her grief she had whispered, 'Take courage Charlotte. Take courage'.[14] Anne was buried on the Wednesday in the churchyard of St Mary's parish church, overlooking the sea, Charlotte having decided that she must spare her father the distress of burying three of his children in just nine months.

EIGHT

THE MATURE NOVELIST, 1849–52

' It is over. Branwell – Emily – Anne are gone like dreams – gone as Maria and Elizabeth went twenty years ago. One by one I have watched them fall asleep on my arm – and closed their glazed eyes . . .'.[1]

At her father's suggestion, Charlotte travelled with the faithful Ellen from Scarborough to Filey and then on to Bridlington. Finally, on 20 June 1849, Charlotte set out for Haworth. Her homecoming was heartwrenching. The Parsonage was clean and bright and the dogs, welcoming Charlotte, looked around eagerly for those who had been so long absent. After spending some time with her father, Charlotte retreated to the dining room and broke down under the weight of desolation and bitterness. It was here that she and her sisters had spent so much time writing and discussing their plans, walking around the table as they did so. Martha Brown was to recall how it upset her tremendously to hear Charlotte continuing this habit, walking on and on alone at night. Charlotte also dreamed of her lost family, unable to recall them in health and seeing them instead in their last illnesses.

There was only one way to dull the pain: Charlotte picked up her writing again. She had been working on her new novel, *Shirley*, since late in December 1847 but the task had been interrupted by the recent tragedies. Now Charlotte had no one with whom to discuss her work; the creative support had evaporated and she felt she was fabricating her tale, 'darkly in the silent workshop of [her] own brain'.[2] The manuscript of the novel reveals her distress and doubts, for it is less assured than *Jane Eyre*, containing many more deletions and alterations.[3] The focus is ill-defined and the attention shifts from Caroline Helstone to Shirley Keeldar, a character whom Charlotte admitted was based on how Emily might have been, had her circumstances been different. At this time Charlotte was almost obsessive about her own health and that of her elderly father and Ellen, not unnaturally fearing the consequences of every slight indisposition. Correspondence with George Smith and William Smith Williams in London now provided the intellectual companionship she craved and her long-standing correspondence with Ellen supplied friendly support and local gossip.

The manuscript of *Shirley* was collected by James Taylor of Smith, Elder & Co. on 8 September 1849. She was relieved when Williams responded positively. However, Smith, Elder & Co. rejected the bitterly sarcastic preface she had penned for *Shirley*, in which she attacked the *Quarterly Review*'s unsigned review of *Jane Eyre*.[4] Charlotte pondered whether she should forgo her anonymity now that her two very private sisters were dead but for the time being she preferred the protection of her pseudonym. She confessed to Williams that in creating Currer Bell, she felt like a wizard who had created a particularly powerful spirit. Mary Taylor, safely in New Zealand, had shared the secret for some time, Ellen had been told officially after Emily's death, though she probably knew before, and Mr Brontë had been admitted to the secret early in 1848 when the sisters' first three novels had achieved success.

Shirley was published under Charlotte's pseudonym on 26 October 1849. Reviews were mixed. Currer Bell's second novel did not receive the enthusiastic praise of *Jane Eyre*. Critics again praised the author's power and originality but thought the story weak and the first chapter vulgar and unnecessary. They also now believed beyond doubt that Currer Bell was a woman. Charlotte was wounded by G.H. Lewes's attack on *Shirley* in the *Edinburgh Review* of January 1850[5] in which he revealed that Currer Bell was the spinster daughter of a clergyman and criticized her style for wandering into vulgarities that would be inexcusable even in a man. She found his review 'brutal and savage' and confessed to Williams that it had made her feel 'cold and sick'.[6] Charlotte had sent copies of *Shirley* to the novelists Elizabeth Gaskell and Harriet Martineau, whom she admired, and had struck up a correspondence with them, though retaining her anonymity.

George Smith and William Smith Williams had tried to persuade their notorious author to visit them in London many times but the succession of family bereavements and now her own familiarity with solitude had prevented her. However, by the end of the year, she was ready to escape the confines of Haworth and accepted George Smith's invitation to stay at his mother's home. While there she was extremely hurt by a *Times* review of *Shirley* which branded the book 'commonplace and puerile'.[7] The highlight of her visit to London in late November and early December of 1849 was her encounter with her hero, William Makepeace Thackeray, author of *Vanity Fair* (1847), though Charlotte was so consumed with shyness and awe that she said little. On a different occasion Charlotte also met several eminent literary critics, whom she found pompous and arrogant, thus removing her fear of them, and Harriet Martineau, the author of *Deerbrook* (1839), who was moved by Miss Brontë's recent tragedies.

Ellen came to stay over the Christmas period and must have been a great support. Charlotte explained her feelings for Ellen to William Smith Williams: 'no new friend, however lofty or profound in intellect . . . could be to me what Ellen is . . . she is without romance . . . but she is good – she is true – she is faithful and I love her.'[8]

At the end of January, Mr Brontë's curate, Arthur Bell Nicholls, had somehow discovered the identity of the author of *Jane Eyre* and *Shirley* and, having read the latter, was delighted, roaring with laughter at the scenes featuring the curates, even though he was caricatured as the Irish curate Mr MacCarthey. The following month all of Haworth knew that they had a famous author in their midst and the villagers were clamouring to borrow the books from the Mechanics' Institute Library. Charlotte was both acutely embarrassed and flattered by the attention, and also touched by the kind and simple tributes she received from ordinary people. On 22 February she noted that the first tourists had begun to arrive in the village, anxious to seek out Currer Bell, and by the end of the month the *Bradford Observer* revealed her identity further abroad.

By the dark early months of 1850, Charlotte had become depressed as the reality of her lonely future began to sink in and it is clear that she had come to rely on the stimulation of letters, packages of books and the glamour of contact with literary London. Smith, Elder & Co. had become what Mary Taylor, writing to Elizabeth Gaskell in 1857,[9] felt that Charlotte saw as 'a passport to the society of clever people'. Mr Brontë insisted that she accept invitations from the likes of Sir James Kay Shuttleworth and Charlotte had to admit that the change did much to lift her spirits. Her father was tremendously proud of his only remaining child; Charlotte wrote to him regularly to tell him about her visits to London and her encounters with famous people. Part of her enjoyed her literary fame, while inside she still shrank from new people and situations. Famous now herself, she received enquiries from young aspiring writers, just as she had once written to Robert Southey.

In June Charlotte stayed with the Smiths in London again, dining with Thackeray and sitting for her portrait by George Richmond. Her friendship with George Smith had developed into a valuable business association for both parties, but they also enjoyed each other's company and they exchanged regular, bantering letters. When Ellen heard that Charlotte planned to travel to Edinburgh with George Smith for a holiday, she could not but wonder whether a romance was brewing between her friend and the handsome young publisher. Charlotte was quick, perhaps overly anxious, to correct any misapprehension, telling Ellen that she

and 'George' understood each other fully and that
her eight years of seniority were a perfect safeguard
against any misinterpretation. Smith admired
Charlotte's fine eyes and intellect but she was
unconventional in appearance and he would be
expected to marry someone more suited to his
standing. One wonders if, in her loneliness,
Charlotte attached herself a little too closely to
George Smith, covering up any deeper feelings with
humour. Their friendship never recovered from her
portrayal of him as Dr John in her third novel,
Villette, and when he informed her that he was to be
married she sent him a very terse note of congrat-
ulation. However, the trip to Edinburgh was a great
success. Charlotte particularly enjoyed visiting
Abbotsford, the former home of Walter Scott,
whose novels Charlotte had worshipped as a teen-
ager. On her return home, Charlotte was miserable
now that the excitement had died down, and both
Ellen and Charlotte's father wondered about the
depth of her relationship with Smith. Not long
afterwards he sent Richmond's portrait of Charlotte
as a present for her father, together with an
engraved picture of the Duke of Wellington. He
dismissed Charlotte's thanks by attributing his

generosity to good business practice. As she had done with Heger, perhaps Charlotte was becoming too fond of Smith.

In August 1850 Charlotte accepted the invitation from Sir James and Lady Kay Shuttleworth to stay at Briery Close, Windermere, and it was there that she met Elizabeth Gaskell. The two women were delighted with each other, though Gaskell found Charlotte's tragic life a fascinating source of gossip, which was to taint her portrayal of her friend in the *Life* a few years later.

The autumn saw Charlotte immersed in the painful task of editing her sisters' poems and writing a biographical introduction to a new, one-volume edition of *Wuthering Heights* and *Agnes Grey*. She saw this as a duty to the dead, to clear the soil deposited by the critics and gossipmongers on their graves since their deaths. Thus her editing was quite severe and her presentation of her sisters calculated to swing public opinion in both their favours. Emily and Anne, both educated in the Classics, became naïve artists who spoke from the heart and told the truth about the barbarity around them on the wild moors. The decline of Branwell, though he was not named, became source material for their novels.

This image of Emily and Anne was continued by Elizabeth Gaskell in 1857. Unforgivably, Charlotte condemned *The Tenant of Wildfell Hall* in the 1850 Biographical Notice as 'an entire mistake' and the novel was ignored until recent years.

In December 1850 Charlotte visited Harriet Martineau at the Knoll, Ambleside, and in May and June 1851 she visited London again, this time attending a series of lectures given by Thackeray and marvelling at the Great Exhibition. On her way back from London she stayed with Elizabeth Gaskell at her home at Plymouth Grove, Manchester, and then began writing her third novel to be accepted for publication, *Villette*.

NINE

MARRIAGE AND DEATH, 1852–61

Throughout 1852, Charlotte struggled with depression, ill health and loneliness as she tried to complete *Villette*. When she eventually sent the manuscript to Smith, Elder & Co., it was with a suggestion that the book appear anonymously. This would be the first book to be published with her identity known and she feared the possible comments on the school scenes, which she based on her Brussels experiences. She was anxious for some response from her publishers, for it was also the first book she had written without her sisters being around to offer advice.

In December 1852 Charlotte received a proposal of marriage from Arthur Bell Nicholls. She turned him down but was moved by a level of emotion within him which she had never suspected. He shook from head to foot as he asked for her hand

and spoke of the suffering he endured for months as he doubted her response. Their friendship had developed of late, since Mr Brontë had suffered a mild stroke which necessitated his curate taking on more of the work of the parish, but she did not feel able to give him the answer he requested, because her father was vehemently angry. She felt the injustice of this anger, which was directed at Mr Nicholls's intentions, and this probably made her more sympathetic to his plight.

Villette was published in January 1853 and relations between Charlotte and George Smith were now cool and businesslike. The novel was received with praise and indeed it is Charlotte's most finished, complex and mature work. In April Charlotte spent a week with Elizabeth Gaskell at her home in Manchester.

Arthur Bell Nicholls resigned his curacy at Haworth in May; the villagers contributed to a watch as a testimonial on his departure in August. The following month Elizabeth Gaskell came to stay with Charlotte and Mr Brontë. Charlotte had been corresponding with Mr Nicholls for some time and in January 1854, when he came to stay with Joseph Brett Grant, the curate of nearby Oxenhope, he met

Charlotte several times. By April Mr Brontë had been persuaded to accept the marriage and in June Mr Nicholls returned to Haworth as curate. Ellen was not happy about the union, however, for she had grown close to Charlotte since the deaths of Emily and Anne and feared their friendship slipping away, firstly because of Charlotte's literary fame and new friends, and now because of the demands of a relationship with a man.

Prior to her wedding, Charlotte drew up a marriage settlement, probably to reassure her father that her fiancé had no designs on her money. At the time the deed was drawn up, Charlotte's assets were valued at over £1,600, a considerable sum at the time, which she had saved from payments received for her novels and investments. Until the introduction of the Married Women's Property Act of 1882, on marriage all a woman's possessions passed to her husband, a situation that Anne had explored in *The Tenant of Wildfell Hall*. Charlotte made plans for the wedding, keeping the ceremony itself as quiet and private as possible, and inviting a few more people to the wedding breakfast.

Charlotte and Arthur Bell Nicholls were married on 29 June 1854, early in the morning at Haworth church. The service was conducted by the Revd Sutcliffe Sowden and Miss Wooler gave Charlotte away as Mr Brontë felt unable to attend at the last minute, perhaps distraught at the thought of his only child leaving him and pondering the dangerous consequences which might result should his tiny, 38-year-old daughter become pregnant. Charlotte wore a simple white muslin dress and a green and white bonnet with a veil. Villagers recalled that she looked like 'a little snowdrop'. Her going-away dress was an elegant lavender-striped silk two-piece. The newlyweds travelled to Conway in Wales, and then on to Holyhead where they caught the ferry to Dublin, Mr Nicholls's old university town. There they were met by some of his family before taking a tour of Ireland. Charlotte was delighted and very impressed with her new relatives, whom she found cultured and kind. Mr Nicholls was seen in a different light in his home country and he soared in her estimation. She was still to find that his appreciation of the arts was nothing like her own but now she could tease him about it. Her expectations of marriage were subdued; having become so used to loneliness and illness it came as something of a shock to Charlotte to find her husband congenial and caring and that she actually enjoyed being married. However, Charlotte had been troubled with a cold throughout the honeymoon and was glad to return home. She had also begun to write again and her unfinished fragment *Emma* was published posthumously in 1860, with an introduction by Thackeray.

Charlotte was unexpectedly happy in her marriage and the role of wife kept her very busy. However, returning from a walk on the moor with her husband, Charlotte caught a chill and then became nauseous. A 'natural cause' was ascribed to this but it soon developed into something more severe. She suffered terrible sickness and couldn't digest her food. In February 1855 she changed her will in favour of Mr Nicholls and reassured Ellen and her friends about their devotion to each other: 'I find in my husband the tenderest nurse, the kindest support – the best earthly comfort that ever woman had.'[1] There is no doubt that Charlotte Brontë had found happiness and now, cruelly, it was being taken from her. Charlotte's last letters written from her sickbed are brief, faintly pencilled notes to friends. She became too ill to continue any sort of correspondence, and so her husband wrote on her behalf. As the end approached, Mr Nicholls was too overcome with grief and Mr Brontë wrote to Ellen to prepare her for the worst.

Charlotte Brontë died on 31 March 1855 at the age of thirty-eight. Her last words, on hearing her husband praying that she might be spared were, 'Oh, I am not going to die, am I? He will not separate us, we have been so happy.'[2]

The exact cause of Charlotte's death is uncertain. She was in the early stages of pregnancy and modern scholars have suggested that the cause may have been *Hyperemesis gravidarum*, excessive vomiting in pregnancy which causes dehydration, a condition that is curable today. Ellen came over for the funeral, where the atmosphere was somewhat uneasy because she had felt excluded from the last months of her friend's life.

The bereaved father and husband remained together at the Parsonage for another six years, Mr Nicholls carrying out the more strenuous duties and the two men drawn together, comforting each other in their grief. Troubled by the inaccuracy of some of the obituaries and press accounts that were appearing, Mr Brontë contacted Elizabeth Gaskell to ask if she would consider writing an account of his daughter's life in order to set the record straight. Ironically, some of this misinformation originated from Gaskell herself, from letters she had written to friends. However, she visited Haworth in 1855 and set about her task with energy and some trepidation, acknowledging that she was a novelist, not a biographer. She travelled to Brussels and spoke to Constantin Heger, had extensive help from Ellen Nussey, and contacted Mary Taylor, Martha Brown and as many people as she could who had known the Brontës. She had the unique advantage for a Brontë biographer of having known her subject and access to both Mr Brontë and Mr Nicholls, though she did not use them as much as she might have done, probably feeling that their sensitivities might be bruised. Thus she obtained much of her information from Ellen, who was not neutral when it came to the men in Charlotte's life.

Two years later *The Life of Charlotte Brontë*, published by Smith, Elder & Co., appeared. Gaskell's powerful picture of the Brontës has affected subsequent interpretations of the family. The publication of the *Life* increased the number of visitors to Haworth and Mr Brontë and Mr Nicholls replied to requests for examples of Charlotte's handwriting by cutting small fragments from some of her letters.

Patrick Brontë died on 7 June 1861, at the age of eighty-four, after suffering convulsions and lapsing into unconsciousness; his son-in law and Martha Brown were in attendance. His funeral took place on 12 June and the shops in Haworth were closed as a mark of respect. The church was packed with mourners and several hundred more remained outside to pay tribute to the only incumbent of Haworth most of them had known. Special permission was obtained so that the old man could be interred with his wife, Maria, Elizabeth, Elizabeth (Aunt) Branwell, Branwell, Emily and Charlotte in the family vault. The vault was sealed and the clergyman who had served the village faithfully for over forty years, and presided over the world's most remarkable literary family, was laid to rest.

NOTES

INTRODUCTION

1. Review of *The Tenant of Wildfell Hall*, E.P. Whipple, 'Novels of the Season', *North American Review*, cxli, October 1848, pp. 354–69, in Miriam Allott (ed.), *Critical Heritage: The Brontës* (London, Routledge & Kegan Paul, 1974), p. 261.

2. Review of *Jane Eyre* in *Atlas*, 23 October 1847, p. 719, in Allott, *Critical Heritage*, p. 68.

3. Charlotte Brontë to Ellen Nussey, 4 February 1850, in T.J. Wise and J.A. Symington (eds), *The Brontës: Their Lives, Friendships and Correspondence* (4 vols, Oxford, Shakespeare Head Press, 1932) (hereafter *SHB L & L*), iii, p. 73.

4. Charlotte Brontë to William Smith Williams, 22 February 1850, *SHB L & L*, iii, p. 80.

5. [G.H. Lewes], review of *Jane Eyre*, *Fraser's Magazine*, December 1847, xxxvi, pp. 686–95, in Allott, *Critical Heritage*, p. 84.

CHAPTER ONE

1. Drumballeyroney parish records, quoted in J. Horsfall Turner, *Brontëana: The Rev. Patrick Brontë, his Collected Works and Life* (Bingley, T. Hanson, 1898), p. 284.

2. Admissions Registers 1802–35, St John's College, Cambridge, MS C4.5, no. 1235, quoted in Barker, *Letters*, p. 835.

3. Turner, *Brontëana*, 1898.

4. Anne Brontë to the Revd David Thom, 30 December 1848, quoted in Barker, *Letters*, pp. 220–2.

5. Maria Branwell to Patrick Brontë, 21 October 1812, *SHB L & L*, i, pp. 18–19.

6. Maria Branwell to Patrick Brontë, 18 November 1812, Barker, *Letters*, p. 55, Brotherton Library, University of Leeds.

7. Elizabeth Firth, diary, original manuscript held at Sheffield University Library.

8. Patrick Brontë, 'Cottage Poems' in Turner, *Brontëana*, p. 19.

9. 'Cottage Poems', 1811; 'The Rural Minstrel', 1813; 'The Cottage in the Wood', 1815; 'The Maid of Killarney', 1818 all in Turner, *Brontëana*.

10. Maria Brontë, 'The Advantages of Poverty in Religious Concerns', Brotherton Library, University of Leeds.

CHAPTER TWO

1. Babbage, Benjamin Herschel, *Report to the General Board of Health of a Preliminary Enquiry into . . . the Hamlet of Haworth*, London, W. Clowes & Sons for HMSO, 1850.

2. *Wuthering Heights*, chapter 1.

3. Emily Brontë, 'A little while, a little while', 4 December 1838, Honresfeld Manuscript. The present whereabouts of this MS, formerly in the collection of Sir Alfred Law and William Law, is unknown.

4. Quoted by Elizabeth Gaskell to Catherine Winkworth, 25 August 1850, in J.A.V. Chapple and A. Pollard, *The Letters of Mrs Gaskell* (Manchester, Manchester University Press, 1966), p. 124.

5. Cowan Bridge Registers, Cumbria District Archives.

6. Ibid.

CHAPTER THREE

1. Charlotte Brontë, St Martin's Parsonage, Birmingham, Roe Head Album, Brontë Parsonage Museum (hereafter BPM): C108.

2. Anne, Emily and Charlotte Brontë, *c.* 1834, by Branwell Brontë, National Portrait Gallery, London.

3. The original complete portrait featured the three sisters and Branwell, who held what appears to be a gun. A very poor quality early photograph of this 'gun group' portrait has survived, BPM: Mildred G. Christian Collection.

4. Emily Brontë by Branwell Brontë, National Portrait Gallery.

5. Christine Alexander and Jane Sellars, *The Art of the Brontës* (Cambridge, Cambridge University Press, 1995), pp. 25–6, 52.

CHAPTER FOUR

1. Charlotte Brontë, Roe Head Journal, BPM: Bon 98.

2. Robert Southey to Charlotte Brontë, March 1837, BPM: BS X, S.

Notes

3. Branwell Brontë and Patrick Brontë to William Robinson, 16 November 1835, BPM: BS 134.5.

4. Patrick Brontë to John Driver, 23 February 1838, BPM: BS 185.5.

CHAPTER FIVE

1. Emily Brontë diary paper, 30 July 1845, *SHB, L&L*, ii, pp. 50–1.

2. Anne Brontë diary paper, 31 July 1845, *SHB, L&L*, ii, pp. 52–3.

3. *Jane Eyre*, Chapter 20.

4. The apostles cupboard from North Lees Hall is now in the Brontë Parsonage Museum.

5. Charlotte Brontë to Ellen Nussey, 31 July 1845, BPM: Gr E 7.

6. Branwell Brontë to Francis Grundy, October 1845, Brotherton Library, University of Leeds, in Barker, *Letters*, p. 137.

7. Branwell Brontë to Joseph Bentley Leyland, *c.* June–July 1846, in *Leyland Manuscripts*, pp. 33–4. The *Leyland Manuscripts* are privately printed transcripts of letters from Branwell Brontë to J.B. Leyland, J.A. Symington, *Patrick Branwell Brontë: A Complete Transcript of the Leyland Manuscripts*, privately printed, 1925.

8. Branwell Brontë to J.B. Leyland, 4 August 1845, in *Leyland Manuscripts*, p.17.

9. Branwell Brontë, 'A PARODY', *c.* 22 July 1848, BPM: B28.

10. Charlotte Brontë, 'Biographical Notice of Ellis and Acton Bell', first published in the 1850 edition of *Wuthering Heights* and *Agnes Grey* and reprinted in most modern editions of *Wuthering Heights*.

11. Ibid.

12. *Critic*, 4 July 1846, pp. 6–8, in Allott, *Critical Heritage*, pp. 59–60.

13. *Athenaeum*, 4 July 1846, p. 682, Allott, in *Critical Heritage*, p. 61.

14. Branwell Brontë to J.B. Leyland, 10 September 1845, in *Leyland Manuscripts*, pp. 18–19.

CHAPTER SIX

1. *Atlas*, 23 October 1847, p. 719, in Allott, *Critical Heritage*, pp. 67–8.

2. A.W. Fonblanque, *Examiner*, 27 November 1847, pp. 756–7, in Allott, *Critical Heritage*, p. 76.

3. *Era*, 14 November 1847, p. 9, in Allott, *Critical Heritage*, p. 79.

4. *People's Journal*, November 1847, in Allott, *Critical Heritage*, p. 81.

5. [G.H. Lewes], *Fraser's Magazine*, xxxvi, December 1847, pp. 686–95, in Allott, *Critical Heritage*, p. 85.

6. [Elizabeth Rigby], 'Vanity Fair and Jane Eyre', *Quarterly Review*, lxxxiv, December 1848, pp. 153–85, in Allott, *Critical Heritage*, pp. 105–11.

7. *Athenaeum*, 25 December 1847, pp. 1,324–5, in Allott, *Critical Heritage*, p. 218.

8. *Examiner*, January 1848, pp. 21–2, in Allott, *Critical Heritage*, p. 220.

9. *Britannia*, 15 January 1848, pp. 42–3, in Allott, *Critical Heritage*, p. 224.

10. Thomas Cautley Newby to 'Dear Sir', 15 February 1848, BPM: Bon 1.

11. Charlotte Brontë to Mary Taylor, July 1848, in Joan Stevens (ed.), *Mary Taylor, Friend of Charlotte Brontë: Letters from New Zealand and elsewhere* (Auckland, Auckland University Press, 1972), p. 178.

12. Anne Brontë, Preface to the Second Edition of *The Tenant of Wildfell Hall*, 22 July 1848.

13. Branwell Brontë to John Brown, Sunday, Noon, n.d., Brotherton Collection, University of Leeds.

14. Charlotte Brontë to William Smith Williams, 2 October 1848, Pierpont Morgan Library, New York.

CHAPTER SEVEN

1. Branwell Brontë to J.B. Leyland, 22 July 1848, *Leyland Manuscripts*, Brotherton Collection, University of Leeds, p. 47.

2. Ibid.

3. Francis H. Grundy, *Pictures of the Past, Memories of Men I have Met & Places I have seen* (London, Griffith & Farrar, 1879), p. 91.

4. Francis A. Leyland, *The Brontë Family* (2 vols, London, Hurst & Blackett, 1886), ii, pp. 278–9.

5. Charlotte Brontë to William Smith Williams, 2 October 1848, Pierpont Morgan Library, New York.

6. Ibid.

7. Charlotte Brontë to William Smith Williams, 2 November 1848, BPM: BS 66.

8. Charlotte Brontë, 'Biographical Notice', in the 1850 edition of *Wuthering Heights* and *Agnes Grey*.

9. Charlotte Brontë to Ellen Nussey, 19 December 1848, *SHB L & L*, ii, p. 293.

10. In the first biography of Emily, it is stated that she died on the

sofa in the dining room but there is no previous source for this story. Mary Robinson (Agnes Mary Duclaux), *Emily Brontë*, London, Eminent Women's Series, 1883, p. 230; reprinted 1997 by Routledge, London.

10. Ellen Nussey, 'Reminiscences', *Brontë Society Transactions*, 2.10.76 (1898), first published in *Scribner's Magazine*, 1871.

11. Anne Brontë, 'A dreadful darkness closes in', 9 & 28 January 1849, BPM: Bon 137.

12. Ibid.

13. Anne Brontë to Ellen Nussey, 5 April 1849, BPM: BS 5.

14. Ellen Nussey, 'Reminiscences'.

CHAPTER EIGHT

1. Charlotte Brontë to William Smith Williams, 13 June 1849, British Library: Ashley 172.

2. Charlotte Brontë to William Smith Williams, 17 September 1849, BPM: Bon 214.

3. The manuscript of Charlotte's *Shirley*, along with *Jane Eyre* and *Villette*, is now in the British Library in London. *The Professor* is held at the Pierpont Morgan Library, New York, and the unfinished fragment, *Emma*, is at Princeton University, New Jersey. No manuscripts of Emily's or Anne's novels have survived.

4. Charlotte Brontë, 'Word to the "Quarterly"', BPM: Seton-Gordon 96.

5. [G.H. Lewes], *Edinburgh Review*, xci, January 1850, pp. 153–73, in Allott, *Critical Heritage*, p. 160.

6. Charlotte Brontë to William Smith Williams, 10 January 1850, quoted in Barker, p. 614.

7. *The Times*, 7 December 1849, in Allott, *Critical Heritage,* p. 149.

8. Charlotte Brontë to William Smith Williams, 3 January 1850, BPM: BS 73.

9. Stevens, *Mary Taylor*, p. 166.

CHAPTER NINE

1. Charlotte Brontë to Ellen Nussey, 21 February 1855, BPM: BS101.

2. Elizabeth Gaskell, *Life of Charlotte Brontë* (Oxford University Press, 1996), p. 400.

BIBLIOGRAPHY

THE BRONTËS' WORK

Clarendon Editions or World's Classics editions of *Jane Eyre*, *Wuthering Heights*, *Agnes Grey*, *The Tenant of Wildfell Hall*, *Shirley*, *Villette* and *The Professor*, published by Oxford University Press.

Alexander, Christine (ed.) *An Edition of the Early Writings of Charlotte Brontë, 1829–1835*, 2 vols, Oxford, Basil Blackwell, Shakespeare Head Press, 1987–91. In progress.

Barker, Juliet (ed.) *The Brontës: A Life in Letters*, London, Harmondsworth, Viking, 1997.

——. *Charlotte Brontë: Juvenilia 1829–1835*, London, Harmondsworth, Penguin Books, 1996.

——. *The Brontës: Selected Poems*, London, J.M. Dent, 1985.

Chitham, Edward (ed.) *The Poems of Anne Brontë: A New Text and Commentary*, London, Macmillan, 1979.

Gezari, Janet (ed.) *The Poems of Emily Jane Brontë*, London, Harmondsworth, Penguin Books, 1992.

Lonoff, Sue (ed.) *The Belgian Essays: Charlotte and Emily Brontë*, New Haven and London, Yale University Press, 1996.

Neufeldt, Victor A. (ed.) *The Poems of Charlotte Brontë: A New Text and Commentary*, New York, Garland Publishing, 1985.

——. *The Poems of Patrick Branwell Brontë: A New Text and Commentary*, New York, Garland Publishing, 1990.

——. *The Works of Patrick Branwell Brontë: An Edition, Volume I*, New York, Garland Publishing Inc., 1997. In progress.

Smith, Margaret (ed.) *The Letters of Charlotte Brontë, Volume I, 1829–1847*, Oxford, Clarendon Press, 1996. In progress.

Turner, J. Horsfall. *Brontëana: The Rev. Patrick Brontë, his Collected Works and Life*, Bingley, T. Hanson, 1898.

Wise, T.J. and J.A. Symington (eds). *The Brontës: Their Lives, Friendships and Correspondence*, 4 vols, Oxford, Basil Blackwell, Shakespeare Head Press, 1932.

THE BRONTËS' LIVES

Alexander, Christine. *The Early Writings of Charlotte Brontë*, Oxford, Basil Blackwell, 1983.

Barker, Juliet. *The Brontës*, London, Weidenfeld & Nicolson, 1994.

Chadwick, Esther Alice. *In the Footsteps of the Brontës*, London, Pitnam and Sons, 1914.

Chitham, Edward. *A Life of Anne Brontë*, Oxford, Basil Blackwell, 1991.

Du Maurier, Daphne. *The Infernal World of Branwell Brontë*, London, Harmondsworth, Penguin Books, 1972.

Fraser, Rebecca. *Charlotte Brontë*, London, Methuen, 1988.

Gaskell, Elizabeth. *The Life of Charlotte Brontë*, Oxford, Oxford University Press, 1996.

Gerin, Winifred. *Anne Brontë*, London, Thomas Nelson, 1959.

——. *Branwell Brontë*, London, Thomas Nelson, 1961.

——. *Charlotte Brontë: The Evolution of Genius*, Oxford, Clarendon Press, 1967.

——. *Emily Brontë: A Biography*, Oxford, Clarendon Press, 1971.

Bibliography

Langland, Elizabeth. *Anne Brontë: The Other One*, Basingstoke, Macmillan Education Ltd, 1989.

Lock, John & W.T. Dixon. *A Man of Sorrow: The Life, Letters and Times of the Revd Patrick Brontë*, London, Thomas Nelson and Sons, 1965.

Whitehead, Barbara. *Charlotte Brontë and her 'dearest Nell': The Story of a Friendship*, Otley, Smith Settle, 1993.

FURTHER READING

Alexander, Christine & Jane Sellars. *The Art of the Brontës*, Cambridge, Cambridge University Press, 1995.

Allott, Miriam (ed.). *The Brontës: The Critical Heritage*, London, Routledge & Kegan Paul, 1974.

Brontë Society Transactions, Haworth, 1898–present.

Chapple, J.A.V. & Pollard, Arthur. *The Letters of Mrs. Gaskell*, Manchester, Manchester University Press, 1966.

Chitham, Edward & Winnifrith, Tom. *Brontë Facts and Brontë Problems*, London, The Macmillan Press Ltd, 1983.

Davies, Stevie. *Emily Brontë: Heretic?*, London, The Women's Press Ltd, 1994.

Ewbank, Inga Stina. *Their Proper Sphere: A Study of the Brontë Sisters as early-Victorian female Novelists*, London, Edward Arnold, 1966.

Grundy, Francis H. *Pictures of the Past, Memories of Men I have Met & Places I Have Seen*, London, Griffith & Farrar, 1879.

Leyland, Francis A. *The Brontë Family*, London, Hurst & Blackett, 1886, 2 vols.

O'Neill, Jane. *The World of the Brontës*, London, Carlton Books, 1997.

Stevens, Joan (ed.). *Mary Taylor, Friend of Charlotte Brontë:*

Bibliography

Letters from New Zealand and Elsewhere, Auckland, Auckland University Press, 1972.

Stoneman, Patsy. *Brontë Transformations: The Cultural Dissemination of* Jane Eyre *and* Wuthering Heights, London, Harvester Wheatsheaf, 1996.

POCKET BIOGRAPHIES

For a copy of our complete list or details of other Sutton titles, please
contact Emma Leitch at Sutton Publishing Limited, Phoenix Mill,
Thrupp, Stroud, Gloucestershire, GL5 2BU